THE NEW TEEN TITANS

VOLUME
FIVE

THE NEW TEEN TITANS

VOLUME **FIVE**

WRITTEN BY
MARV WOLFMAN

ART BY
GEORGE PÉREZ
and
ROMEO **TANGHAL**
with
PABLO **MARCOS**

COVER ART BY
GEORGE **PÉREZ**

THE NEW TEEN TITANS
CREATED BY
MARV **WOLFMAN**
AND
GEORGE **PÉREZ**

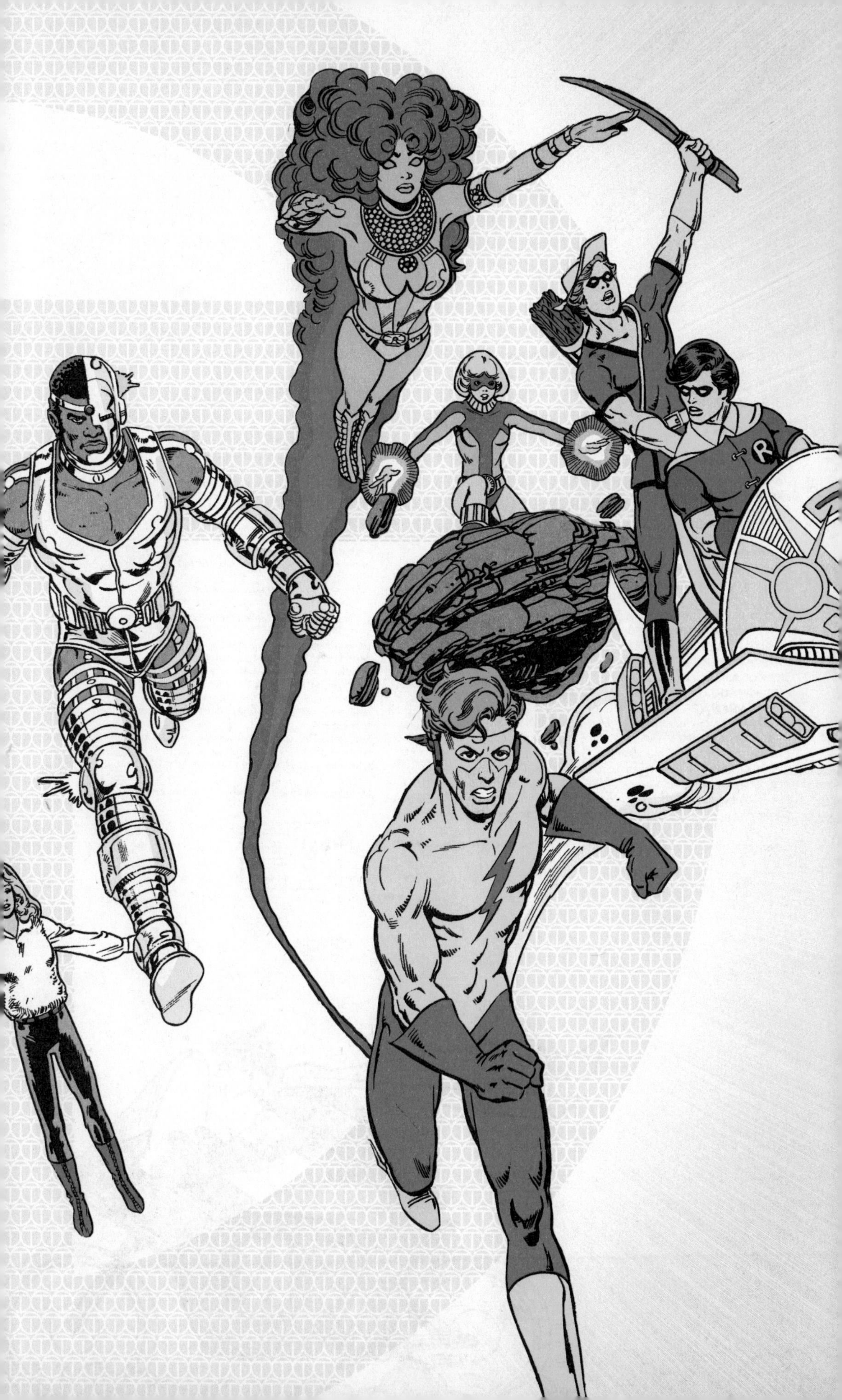

LEN **WEIN** Editor – Original Series
JEB **WOODARD** Group Editor – Collected Editions
SCOTT **NYBAKKEN** Editor – Collected Edition
STEVE **COOK** Design Director – Books
CURTIS **KING JR.** Publication Design

BOB **HARRAS** Senior VP – Editor-in-Chief, DC Comics

DIANE **NELSON** President
DAN **DIDIO** and JIM **LEE** Co-Publishers
GEOFF **JOHNS** Chief Creative Officer
AMIT **DESAI** Senior VP – Marketing & Global Franchise Management
NAIRI **GARDINER** Senior VP – Finance
SAM **ADES** VP – Digital Marketing
BOBBIE **CHASE** VP – Talent Development
MARK **CHIARELLO** Senior VP – Art, Design & Collected Editions
JOHN **CUNNINGHAM** VP – Content Strategy
ANNE **DEPIES** VP – Strategy Planning & Reporting
DON **FALLETTI** VP – Manufacturing Operations
LAWRENCE **GANEM** VP – Editorial Administration & Talent Relations
ALISON **GILL** Senior VP – Manufacturing & Operations
HANK **KANALZ** Senior VP – Editorial Strategy & Administration
JAY **KOGAN** VP – Legal Affairs
DEREK **MADDALENA** Senior VP – Sales & Business Development
JACK **MAHAN** VP – Business Affairs
DAN **MIRON** VP – Sales Planning & Trade Development
NICK **NAPOLITANO** VP – Manufacturing Administration
CAROL **ROEDER** VP – Marketing
EDDIE **SCANNELL** VP – Mass Account & Digital Sales
COURTNEY **SIMMONS** Senior VP – Publicity & Communications
JIM (SKI) **SOKOLOWSKI** VP – Comic Book Specialty & Newsstand Sales
SANDY **YI** Senior VP – Global Franchise Management

Cover color and interior color reconstruction by **PACIFIC RIM GRAPHICS.**

THE NEW TEEN TITANS VOLUME FIVE
Published by DC Comics. Compilation and all new material Copyright
© 2016 DC Comics. All Rights Reserved. Originally published in single
magazine form in THE NEW TEEN TITANS 28-34 and THE NEW TEEN
TITANS ANNUAL 2. Copyright © 1983 DC Comics. All Rights Reserved.
All characters, their distinctive likenesses and related elements featured in
this publication are trademarks of DC Comics. The stories, characters and
incidents featured in this publication are entirely fictional. DC Comics does
not read or accept unsolicited submissions of ideas, stories or artwork.

DC Comics
2900 West Alameda Ave.
Burbank, CA 91505
Printed by RR Donnelley, Owensville, MO, USA. 6/24/16.
First Printing.
ISBN: 978-1-4012-6358-4

Library of Congress Cataloging-in-Publication Data

Names: Wolfman, Marv, author. | Pérez, George, 1954-
illustrator. | Tanghal, Romeo, illustrator.
Title: New Teen Titans. Volume five / written by Marv
Wolfman ; art by George Pérez and Romeo Tanghal.
Description: Burbank, CA : DC Comics, [2016]
Identifiers: LCCN 2016017547 | ISBN 9781401263584
(paperback)
Subjects: LCSH: Comic books, strips, etc. | BISAC: COMICS &
GRAPHIC NOVELS / Superheroes.
Classification: LCC PN6728.T34 W626 2016 | DDC 741.5/973—
dc23
LC record available at https://lccn.loc.gov/2016017547

TABLE OF CONTENTS

All stories by MARV WOLFMAN,
all cover art and story pencils by GEORGE PÉREZ,
and all story inks by ROMEO TANGHAL, except where noted.

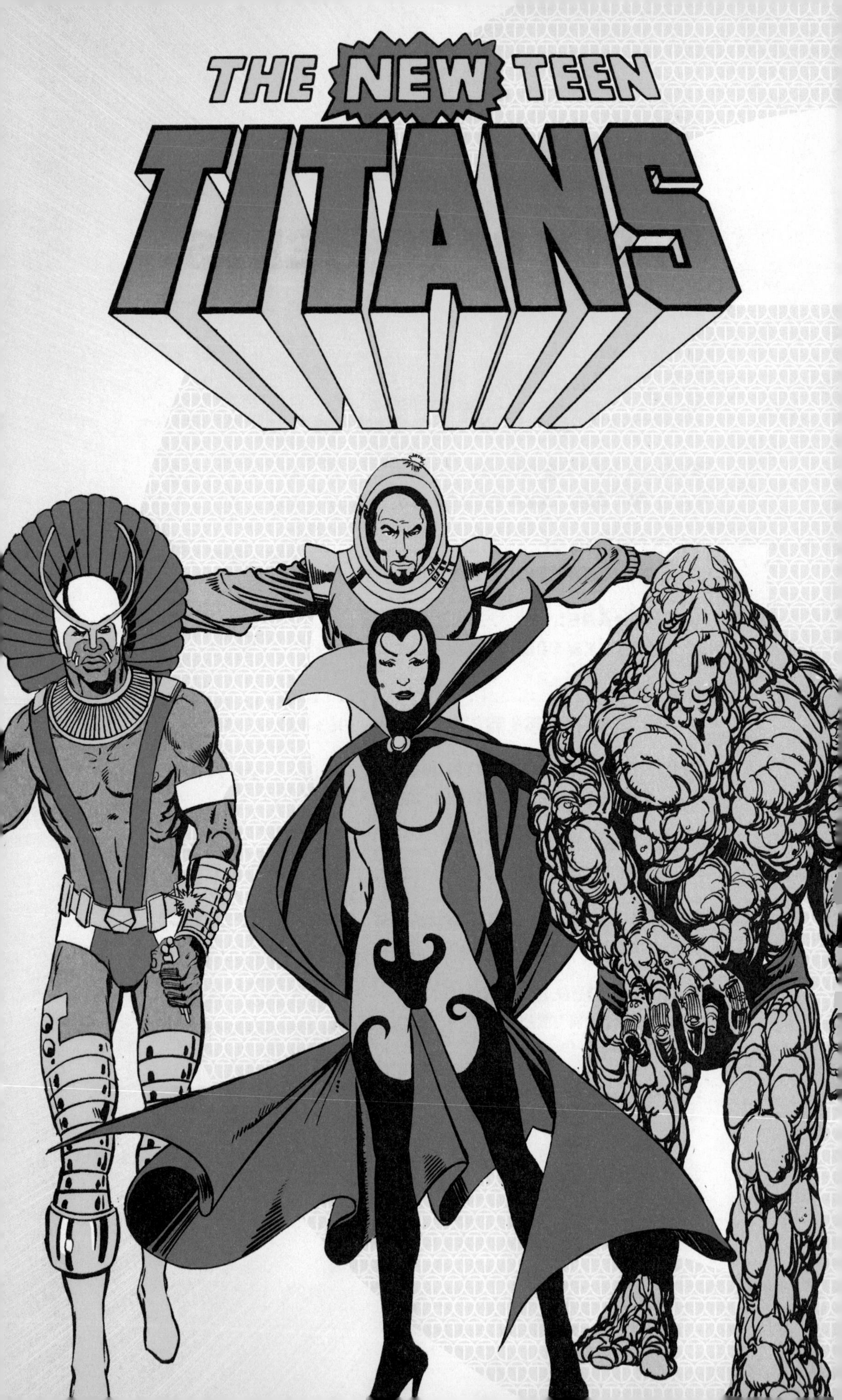
THE NEW TEEN
TITANS

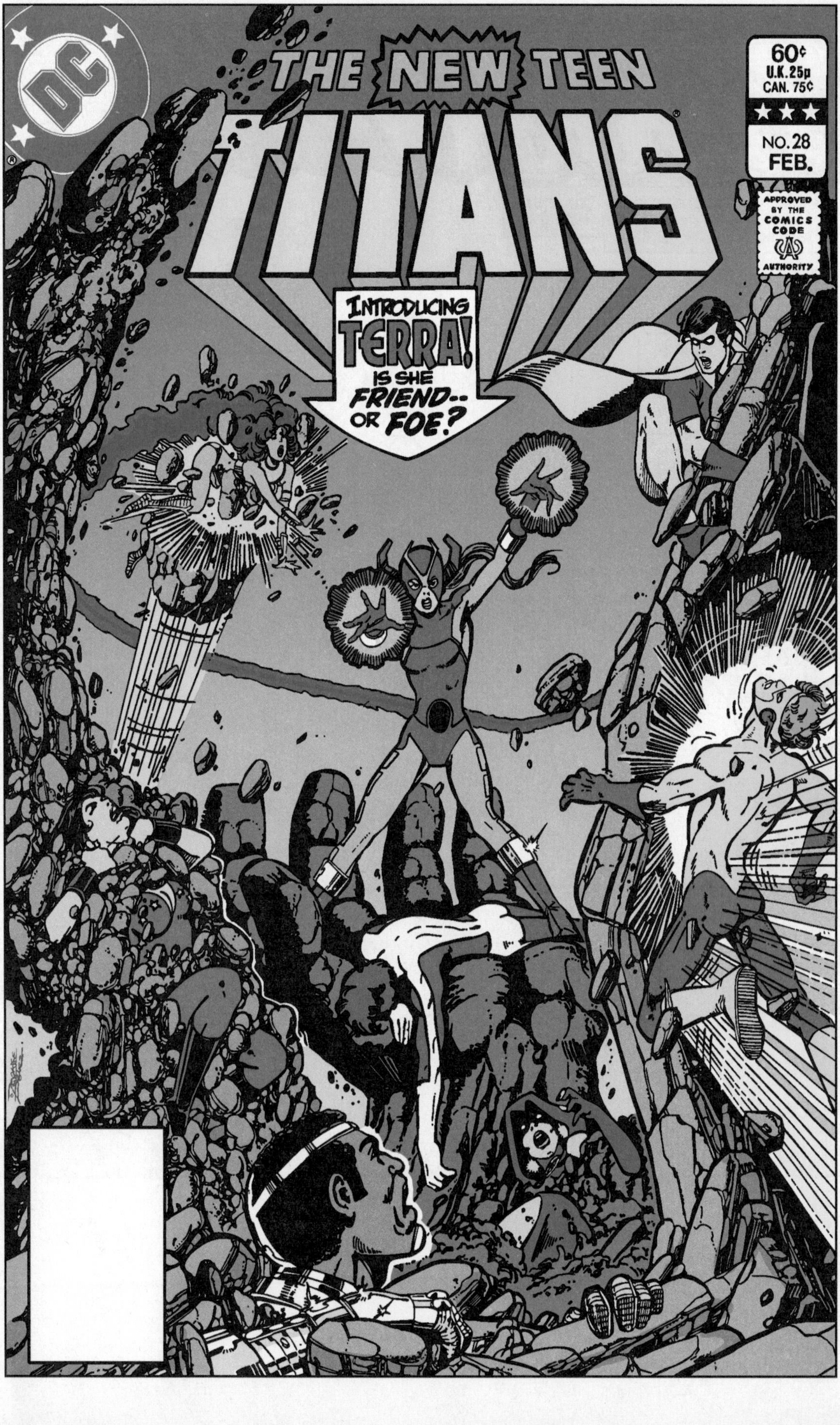
THE NEW TEEN
TITANS
60¢
U.K. 25p
CAN. 75¢
NO. 28
FEB.
APPROVED BY THE COMICS CODE AUTHORITY
INTRODUCING TERRA! IS SHE FRIEND.. OR FOE?

"PUKE-FACE"? *NOW* YOU'VE DONE IT, GORGEOUS. YOU'VE WOUNDED MY FRAGILE *EGO.* YOU'VE CUT ME SEVERELY TO MY EVER-CUTE *QUICK.*

IF I WEREN'T *SANFORIZED,* I'D SHRIVEL UP AND DIE.

YOU *STILL* MAY, CREEP--IF YOU DON'T LEAVE ME ALONE.

HONEY, WITH A FACE LIKE YOURS, I'D FOLLOW YOU *ANYWHERE...*

AT LEAST UNTIL I RECOVER THAT *MONEY* YOU STOLE.

TELL YA WHAT. *FORGET* THIS CRIME JUNK. LET'S CATCH A MOVIE, EAT SOME POPCORN, MAYBE *NECK* A LITTLE...

BOY, YOU DON'T *QUIT,* DO YOU?

I TOLD YOU BEFORE, I *HAVE* TO DO THIS. THERE'S TOO MUCH AT STAKE FOR ME TO STOP.

DON'T YOU THINK I CAN'T *TELL* THAT, TERRA? HEY, HARD AS IT IS TO BELIEVE, I'M *MORE* THAN JUST A GREAT-LOOKING *HUNK.*

I CAN *HELP!* WHAT'S WRONG?

I CAN'T *TELL* YOU, CHANGELING.

AND I'M REALLY *SORRY* I HAVE TO DO THIS--

2

9

--BUT MY *PARENTS'* LIVES ARE AT STAKE!

THEY'LL *DIE* UNLESS I FINISH THIS MISSION.

YOUR *PARENTS?* TERRA. *LISTEN* TO ME... I'M BEING *SERIOUS* NOW.

THE TITANS CAN *HELP.*

NO ONE CAN *HELP* ME, CHANGELING.

I'VE RELIED ON OTHERS FOR *TWO YEARS* AND I'VE ALWAYS FAILED. I'VE *GOT* TO DO THIS MYSELF.

YOU'RE NOT GOING TO GIVE ME THE CHANCE TO PLAY *HERO?*

TERRA, *TERRA, TERRA--* THIS IS WHAT I *LOVE* DOING SECOND MOST IN THE WORLD.

C'MON, WE'LL TEAM UP AND *SAVE* YOUR PARENTS.

I SAID-- **NO!** GO AWAY!

I CAN'T, SWEETS. I'M *STUCK* ON YOU.

YOU IDIOT! LET *GO* OF ME!

I'LL *CRUSH* YOU IF I HAVE TO!

HEY, WAIT! STICKS AND STONES MAY BREAK MY--

AGHHHH!

TERRA? ARE YOU ALL RIGHT?

ONE OF HER OWN STONES *HIT* HER. SHE LOOKS DAZED, *HURT.*

C'MON, BEAUTIFUL-- YOU GOTTA *TALK.*

BLAST, SHE ISN'T *MOVING.* DON'T TELL ME THAT KI--

JERK!

SKODM!

YOU FELL FOR THE *OLDEST* TRICK IN THE WORLD!

SEEYA AROUND, NERD!

TERRA?

TERRA?

I DON'T *LIKE* THIS. SHE'S OBVIOUSLY IN TROUBLE. SHE *NEEDS* MY HELP. SHE NEEDS *ME.*

AND AGAIN I *FAILED.*

I'VE BEEN *USELESS* FOR MONTHS NOW --ALMOST *AFRAID* TO USE MY POWERS TO THEIR FULLEST...

...EVER SINCE WHAT HAPPENED TO *MADAME ROUGE*...EVER SINCE I ACCIDENTALLY KIL--

GAR LOGAN'S THOUGHT FADES AS WE SHIFT EASTWARD...

ZANDIA: A SMALL BALTIC ISLAND. ITS CHIEF EXPORT IS *VIO-LENCE,* FOR ZANDIA IS AN ISLE RUN BY TERRORISTS.

EVEN AS ITS CHURCH IS OPERATED BY THE CULT OF *BROTHER BLOOD,* A MAN WHOM, IT IS SAID, HAS LIVED MORE THAN SEVEN HUNDRED YEARS.

ALL IS SERENE IN HIS CATHEDRAL OF DEATH.

ALL PERIMETERS CLEAR... NOW CHECKING SOUTHERN BORDERS...

4

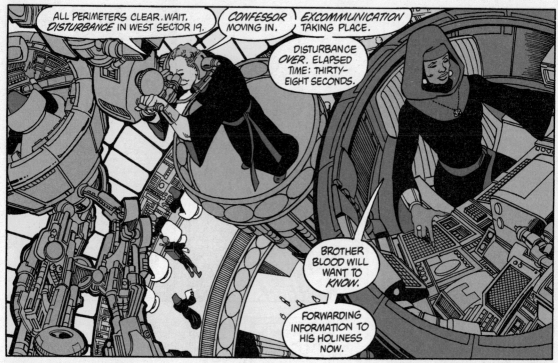

ALL PERIMETERS CLEAR. WAIT. *DISTURBANCE* IN WEST SECTOR 19.

CONFESSOR MOVING IN.

EXCOMMUNICATION TAKING PLACE.

DISTURBANCE OVER. ELAPSED TIME: THIRTY-EIGHT SECONDS.

BROTHER BLOOD WILL WANT TO *KNOW.*

FORWARDING INFORMATION TO HIS HOLINESS NOW.

DELICATE FINGERS DANCE ACROSS THE KEYBOARD.

THEN...

WH-WHAT? HELP!

HER NAME IS *SISTER SADE.* SHE HAS BEEN A LOYAL BELIEVER IN--AND LOVER OF--BROTHER BLOOD FOR THREE YEARS.

IT IS TOO LATE. AT THE AGE OF FOUR, SISTER SADE, THEN HELEN GEARY, DEVELOPED A TERRIBLE FEAR OF SNAKES.

NOW THAT FEAR PROVES HER UNDOING.

SISTER SADE? WHAT *IS* IT? WHAT'S *WRONG?*

WHAT'S SHE DOING?

DON'T YOU SEE THEM? THEY'RE ALL OVER ME. *HELP* ME.

I DON'T SEE *ANYTHING.*

SOMETHING'S *WRONG.* SET ALARMS IMMEDIATELY.

PLEASE-- TAKE THEM OFF ME.

NOW SISTER SOUL TURNS TOWARD THE CONSOLE, READY TO ALERT BROTHER BLOOD'S MERCENARY MISSIONARIES...

I DON'T UNDERSTAND THIS. SHE'S *DEAD*... HER HEART *STOPPED*.

THERE'S NO REPORT OF ANY *BREAK-INS*. NOTHING ON MY *SCANNERS*. I--

SUDDENLY THE GROUND BENEATH HER OPENS, AND SISTER SOUL BEGINS A MILE-LONG FALL

LORD! OH, NO-- NO!

HELP ME! *HELP* ME!

TH-THEY'RE ALL OVER...

STOP HIM! HE'S GOING *CRAZY*!

I'VE GOT TO *STOP THEM*! I'VE GOT TO *KILL THEM*!

BAM BAM

SINCE SHE CAN REMEMBER, SISTER SOUL HAS SUFFERED FROM EXTREME VERTIGO.

HE'S *KILLING* OUR OWN *TROOPS*!

CAN'T HOLD ONTO HIM. HE'S LIKE AN *ANIMAL*!

BAM BAM BAM BAM

NOW HER WORST FEAR HAS COME TO LIFE.

WE HAVE NO *CHOICE*.

CAN'T LET HIM KILL ANYONE *ELSE*!

BAM

BLAM

6

W-WE'VE JUST GOT ORDERS FROM *BROTHER BLOOD.*

IS HE GOING TO *HELP* US?

N-NO... HE SAYS HE'S PREPARING OUR *LAST RITES!*

BUT I DON'T WANT TO *DIE.*

A *SHAME* ZEN, EH, *MONSIEUR?* FOR YOU *WILL.*

ZE *BROTHERHOOD* HAS POWERS MAGNIFIQUE. I, *WARP*, CAN *TWIST SPACE* ITSELF...

...AND SEND YOU MILES AWAY TO YOUR *DOOM*...AT ZE BOTTOM OF ZE *BALTIC SEA.*

DERE DEATHS ARE *EASY*, HERR *WARP.* BUT ZESE FOOLS SHALL FEEL *MY* TERRIBLE POWER.

THE VERY TOUCH OF *PLASMUS* MEANS A BURNING, AGONIZING END.

I HAF BEEN REDUCED TO DIS *PLASMIC MASS.* MY POWERS ARE DARK AND EVIL.

ACH! I *HATE* VHAT I HAF BECOME, BUT I *USE* VHAT I NOW AM FOR DER GOOD OF DER *BROTHERHOOD!*

DERE! YOU ARE REDUCED TO A *PROTOPLASMIC BLOB* EVEN AS I AM--ONLY *YOU* ARE DEVOID OF LIFE.

8

NEW YORK CITY: FAR FROM ZANDIA'S TROUBLED SHORES, BUT SOON TO HAVE ENOUGH TROUBLES OF ITS OWN.

FOR NOW, HOWEVER, THERE IS *PEACE* HERE IN THE PENTHOUSE APARTMENT OF DONNA TROY AND KORY ANDERS...

EVERYTHING SEEMS *PERFECT* BETWEEN YOU AND DICK. I'M SO *GLAD* FOR YOU, KORY.

PERFECT? I DON'T KNOW ABOUT *THAT*, DONNA.

HE'S BEEN ACTING SO *STRANGE* LATELY. SO *TIRED* AND SO...I GUESS *GRUMPY* IS THE WORD.

I WONDER IF HE REALLY *CARES* ABOUT ME? HAVE I DONE SOMETHING *WRONG*?

DON'T PUT YOURSELF DOWN, HONEY. THIS IS *DICK'S* PROBLEM.

I'VE SEEN HIM GO THROUGH THESE TIMES *BEFORE*.

DICK'S *PUSHING* HIMSELF. HE WORKS WITH US, ON HIS OWN, AND HE GOES TO SCHOOL, AND THEN HE WORKS ALONGSIDE THE BATMAN.

AND YOU KNOW HOW HE *FEELS* ABOUT THE BATMAN. HE WANTS TO BE AS *GOOD*...

...EVEN THOUGH HE NEVER *CAN* BE.

HE'S JUST NOT *DRIVEN* THE WAY THE BATMAN IS. HE HASN'T GOT THAT SAME *FANATICAL OBSESSION*.

SO DICK'S ALL *TENSE* TRYING TO DO TOO MANY THINGS AT ONCE. THE BEST *YOU* CAN DO IS GET HIM TO *RELAX*.

I KNOW HE'S *SHORT-TEMPERED* NOW, BUT WHEN HE'S NOT TRYING TO LIVE UP TO SOME IMPOSSIBLE IMAGE--

--HE'S ONE OF THE MOST *WONDERFUL* PEOPLE I KNOW.

WERE *YOU* EVER IN LOVE WITH HIM?

ROMANTICALLY? NO. BUT I LOVE HIM AS ONE OF MY DEAREST *FRIENDS*.

(9)

C'MON, KORY-- ANSWER THE *DOOR.*

ANSWER IT!

BZZZZZ

DICK, YOU'RE *RIGHT ON TIME.*

AREN'T I *ALWAYS?* READY TO GO?

YOU LOOK *TIRED.*

YEAH, WELL, I'VE BEEN DOING SOME WORK AT THE CIRCUS, AND... HEY, THAT'S NOT WHY I CAME HERE. LET'S *GO.*

NO. LET'S *STAY* HERE FOR A CHANGE. WE'RE ALWAYS GOING OUT.

CAN WE *UHH-- RELAX...?* JUST FOR ONE EVENING? I'D MUCH RATHER STAY HOME TONIGHT.

BESIDES, I'M *LEAVING--* SO THE PLACE IS ALL YOURS. TERRY AND I HAVE PLANNED A *NIGHT* OF IT.

HE'LL *NEED* IT. HE'S SPENDING THE DAY WITH HIS *EX-WIFE* AND KID.

YOU'RE LOOKING *GREAT,* DONNA.

I HOPE A CERTAIN *MR. LONG* THINKS THE SAME.

KORY, DON'T *WAIT UP* FOR ME.

YOU TWO HAVE FUN, OH, DICK, I'LL SEE YOU *LATE* TOMORROW TO GO OVER THOSE *PLANS.*

TA TA, CREW.

NOW DON'T DO ANYTHING *I* WOULDN'T DO.

OKAY, WE'RE STAYING HOME. *NOW* WHAT DO WE DO?

OH, SOMEHOW WE'LL THINK OF *SOMETHING.*

10

MEANWHILE, LESS THAN FIFTEEN BLOCKS AWAY, AT THE CENTRAL PARK ZOO...

GET *AWAY* FROM ME. I DON'T WANT ANY OF YOU *FOLLOWING* ME.

DON'T YOU PEOPLE UNDERSTAND? *STAY AWAY!*

SHE'S *SCARED.* STARTING TO LASH OUT AT EVERY-ONE.

TROUBLE IS, HER BEING SCARED COULD MEAN SOMEONE *DIES.*

WELL, HERE GOES GAR LOGAN SCREWING UP HIS COURAGE, AND-- OH, *NO!*

CAGES BLASTED OPEN...THE ANIMALS ARE *ESCAPING!*

BETTER CHANGE *FORM...* EVEN THOUGH I'M GETTING *TIRED...* TOO MANY TRANSFORMATIONS IN TOO SHORT A TIME.

NO *CHOICE* THOUGH. THIS IS PRETTY MUCH GONNA *WIPE ME OUT* FOR THE BETTER PART OF A DAY--

--BUT I'VE GOT TO LEND A HELPING *TRUNK* TO STOP THIS ZOO-CREW FROM GETTING OUTTA HAND.

PARDON ME.

EXCUSE ME.

EXCUSE ME.

SORRY.

11

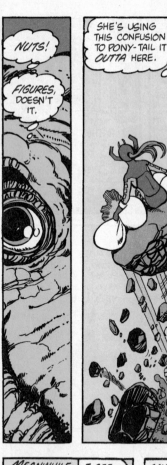

LATER...

WHAT'S *WRONG*, DICK?

OH, NOTHING. SOMETIMES I JUST LIKE BEING *ALONE*.

YOU'D RATHER I WASN'T *HERE*?

OH, NO--*NO.*

DICK, I--

LOOK, I'M SORRY. I HAVE A LOT ON MY *MIND* RIGHT NOW.

DICK, I *LOVE* YOU. I REALLY DO. I--

KORY, PLEASE. I'D RATHER NOT TALK ABOUT *US* RIGHT NOW.

YOU *CARE* FOR ME, DON'T YOU?

OF COURSE. LOOK, I'M *SORRY.* IT'S THAT I HAVEN'T HAD MORE THAN THREE HOURS' *SLEEP* IN THE LAST THREE DAYS--

--AND WHILE YOU WERE IN THE *SHOWER,* I READ THIS NEW COLUMN BY BETHANY SNOW.

SHE'S BLAMING THE *TITANS* FOR EVERYTHING THAT'S *BAD,* WITH THE POSSIBLE EXCEPTION OF THE NEW *TV* SEASON.

I DON'T LIKE *SAYING* THIS, KORY, BUT I'D LOVE TO PLANT MY FIST UP THAT SNOOTY *NOSE* OF HERS.

SNOW STORM
by Bethany Snow

IT'S NOT *YOU,* REALLY. I'M JUST ALL *NERVES* RIGHT NOW.

WOULD YOU LIKE A *BACK RUB?* IT WILL MAKE YOU FEEL BETTER.

KORY--*PLEASE!* DON'T YOU EVER WANT TO ENJOY A *BAD* MOMENT? I JUST WANT TO *THINK.*

AND MAYBE SEE IF *ADRIAN CHASE* HAS CHECKED OUT BETHANY SNOW'S CONNECTIONS WITH *BROTHER BLOOD.*

LET ME *COME* WITH YOU, DICK.

OKAY?

PLEASE?

13

TITANS TOWER, LOCATED IN NEW YORK'S MUDDY EAST RIVER...

INSIDE SITS A YOUNG EMPATH, DEEP IN MEDITATION.

HER NAME IS RAVEN. SHE HAS THE POWER TO TAKE YOUR PAINS AND MAKE THEM HER OWN.

BUT RECENTLY SHE HAS NOT BEEN ABLE TO DISPEL THOSE PAINS. THEY LINGER WITHIN HER. THEY HURT HER. THEY MAY VERY WELL KILL HER.

MEDITATION WIPES AWAY THE FIRST LEVEL OF BEING. SHE REACHES INSIDE HERSELF.

THERE IS A WALL. DARK, MENACING...SO VERY COLD. SHE REACHES FOR THE WALL. REACHES...TOUCHES...

NOK! NOK!

HER TRANCE ENDS, ALL TOO ABRUPTLY.

HI, RAVEN, DID I BOTHER YOU?

N-NO. I... HAVE NOT SEEN YOU FOR AWHILE, WALLACE.

AND I SENSE SOMETHING DISTURBING YOU.

WHAT IS WRONG?

WHAT ELSE? SCHOOL. I'M HAVING TROUBLE STUDYING. YOU HAVE TROUBLES AT YOUR SCHOOL?

IN AZARATH I LEARNED HOW TO STUDY. YOUR SCHOOLS ARE NOT DIFFICULT FOR ME.

MAN, I WISH I COULD SAY THAT. I'M FAILING FRENCH TWO.

AND I CAN'T GIVE UP SCHOOL. I SIMPLY CAN'T.

AND I'M NOT LIKE DICK. I CAN'T JUGGLE HALF A DOZEN PROBLEMS AT ONCE AND STILL DO EVERYTHING SO PERFECTLY.

SOMETIMES I ENVY HIM THAT TALENT.

I CAN'T FOCUS. HALF THE TIME I'M KID FLASH. HALF THE TIME I'M A STUDENT. IT'S NOT WORKING.

14

I NEVER REALLY WANTED TO *BE* KID FLASH, AND I--

HEY! SOMEONE HERE! *HELP!*

HUH?

GARFIELD. HE'S CALLING FOR *HELP.*

WELL, NO PROBLEM *THERE.* I PRESS MY RING AND MY *COSTUME* SHOOTS OUT--

--EXPANDING ON CONTACT WITH THE *AIR.*

SOMETHING *WRONG,* RAVEN? WHY DIDN'T *YOU* *TELEPORT* TO HELP GAR?

I DO NOT TELE-PORT. I MOVE BETWEEN DIM-ENSIONS.

AND GARFIELD'S NEEDS ARE NOT QUITE SO *DESPERATE* AS HE MAKES THEM OUT TO BE.

BUT, MOMENTS LATER...

WELL, WELL, GAR, YOU CAN'T GO CALLING FOR THE TITANS JUST BECAUSE YOU MADE SOME GIRL SWOON.

WHO'S YOUR *FRIEND?*

IS THAT *HER?* THE ONE YOU *TOLD* US ABOUT?

WELL, SHE SURE AIN'T *VALERIE BERTINELLI.*

HIYA, FLEET-FEET. LONG TIME, NO *SEE.*

I ASKED YOU... *WHO'S* THE *GIRL?*

THAT'S NO *GIRL,* THAT'S MY *STRIFE!*

HER NAME'S *TERRA,* LIKE IN EARTH AND GROUND. ONLY IT SHOULD BE *TERROR*-- AS IN-- HOLY COW, WATCH OUT, FELLAS!

SHE'S *HURT,* BUT I CAN *HELP* HER...

HELP? N-NO... DON'T *TOUCH* ME. I KNOW ALL ABOUT YOU.

HEY, CALM DOWN, RAVEN WAS JUST TRYING TO *HELP!*

15

I TOLD YOU BEFORE, JERK-- I DON'T *WANT* HELP.

GET OUTTA MY WAY. LET ME *OUTTA* HERE.

SHE'S *ESCAPING.*

I WILL--

NAH, LET *ME* HANDLE HER, RAVEN.

A LITTLE *SUPER-SPEED VIBRATION* AND I SIPHON OFF THE *AIR* AROUND HER.

SHE GOES DOWN FROM MOMENTARY *LOSS OF OXYGEN.*

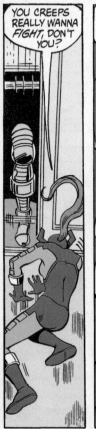

YOU CREEPS REALLY WANNA *FIGHT,* DON'T YOU?

OKAY, I'LL TAKE YOU ALL ON IF I HAV--

OH, NUTS.

I HEARD *SHOUTING.*

WHAT'S *WRONG?*

16

DON'T TELL ME. *YOU'RE* THE REASON MY BEAUTY REST WAS INTERRUPTED.

PUT ME *DOWN*, YOU WALKING GARBAGE CAN!

WHOSE IS SHE, ANYWAY?

GAR FOUND HER. HER NAME'S *TERRA.*

LOGAN? *FIGGERS!*

DON'T TAKE HER TOO *LIGHTLY*, RUST-HEAD. SHE'S *MEANER* THAN SHE LOOKS.

SHE'D *HAVE* TO BE.

OKAY, JERK--YOU *ASKED* FOR IT.

WHAT IN--?

SKRUNCHH

I *WARNED* YOU, DIDN'T I? BUT WOULD YOU *LISTEN*--? *NOOOOO!*

SHE'S GOT POWER OVER THE *EARTH.* AND THAT MEANS MORE 'N JUST MAKING *MUD-PIES!*

POWER ALONE ISN'T ENOUGH TO *STOP* HER.

WE'VE GOT TO *CONVINCE* HER WE CAN HELP.

THERE... CYBORG, *CATCH* HER.

UHHH, THAT *HURTS!*

YOU PLAY WITH *MEAN FRIENDS,* LOGAN.

WATCH IT, TIN-HEAD, I'VE STILL GOT *POWERS.*

WHERE'D YOU *FIND* THIS ONE, ANYWAY? *"HELL-CATS ANONYMOUS"?*

17

TERRA, IT'S REAL DUMB TO KEEP FIGHTING. SO HOW ABOUT GIVING US A CHANCE?

OKAY, OKAY, I BELIEVE. JUST KEEP TWINKLE-TOES AWAY FROM ME.

GOD, I'VE GOT A HEADACHE. WHAT DID YOU DO?

JUST A SUPER-SPEED NERVE PINCH. SORRY.

LISTEN, YOU GOTTA REALIZE, IT'S BEEN A WHILE SINCE I COULD TRUST SOMEBODY.

YOU'RE LOOKING AT ME LIKE I JUST STEPPED OUT OF A PADDED CELL. OKAY, I'LL EXPLAIN.

MY PARENTS... WELL, THEY'RE IN CHARGE OF ANOTHER COUNTRY... AT LEAST MY DAD IS.

I'M SORTA THE NATIONAL EMBARASSMENT. MY REAL MOM DIED IN CHILD-BIRTH, AND I WAS RAISED HERE IN AMERICA SO DAD'S WIFE WOULDN'T HAVE A CORONARY.

'BOUT TWO YEARS AGO I RETURNED TO MY HOMELAND ONLY TO FIND DAD AND GUESS-WHO KIDNAPPED! MY BROTHER, THAT'S BRION, HE AND I SEARCHED FOR THEM...

...ONLY WE GOT SEPARATED 'BOUT THE TIME I RAN ACROSS THESE TERRORISTS WHO SAID THEY WERE HOLDING MY DAD AND THE QUEEN.

THE TERRORISTS THREATENED TO KILL 'EM BOTH IF I DIDN'T USE MY POWERS IN THEIR CAUSE.

I DIDN'T KNOW WHAT ELSE TO DO. BRION WAS OFF SOMEWHERE IN SOUTH AMERICA. I WAS SCARED.

EVERYTHING WILL BE ALL RIGHT, TERRA.

PLEASE, CALL ME TARA, THAT'S MY REAL NAME. THE TERRORISTS THOUGHT IT WAS CUTE TO CALL ME TERRA INSTEAD, 'CAUSE'A MY POWERS.

RAVEN, YOU LOOK LIKE YOU SWALLOWED A PIGEON. SOMETHING WRONG?

IT IS NOTHING... NOTHING.

THOUGH I DO NOT LIKE THESE FEELINGS I SENSE.

OBVIOUSLY YOU WEREN'T BORN WITH YOUR POWERS ...OR WERE YOU?

WHAT DO YOU THINK I AM ANYWAY? SOME KINDA FREAKY MUTANT?

SORRY, TERRA. SAY, HOW OLD ARE YOU ANYWAY?

ALMOST SIXTEEN. HEY, I DON'T LIKE THAT LOOK IN YOUR EYES. I DON'T WANT PITY.

I'VE DON'T PRETTY WELL, CONSIDERING.

LOOK, YOU DON'T WANNA HELP, JUST TELL ME AND I'LL TAKE OFF.

BUT DON'T STARE AT ME LIKE I'M POSTER GIRL FOR "MISS SPAT-UPON OF THE NINETEEN EIGHTIES."

ACROSS TOWN...

DONNA TROY STEPS FROM THE CAB BEFORE TERRY LONG'S APARTMENT. SHE IS VERY HAPPY. DURING THESE PAST MONTHS THEY HAVE BECOME CLOSER THAN SHE EVER FELT SHE COULD BE TO ANYONE.

18

THOUGH BORN MORTAL, SHE WAS RAISED ON PARADISE ISLAND, LEGENDARY HOME OF THE AMAZONS. SHE WAS RAISED AWAY FROM MEN, RAISED TO SOMETIMES *DISTRUST* MEN AND THEIR PROCLIVITIES TOWARD VIOLENCE.

AND FOR MANY YEARS SHE SHARED THAT DISTRUST, UNTIL SHE MET DICK GRAYSON, THEN ROY HARPER, WALLY WEST AND ALL THE OTHERS.

AND, SLOWLY SHE LEARNED TO LOVE.

TERRY, DON'T WORRY, IT'S *ME.*

I LET MYSELF--

OHH, I'M SO *SORRY.*

DONNA? DON'T TELL ME IT'S ALREADY TIME. C'MON *IN.*

WE WERE JUST GOING OVER SOME PAPERS.

YOU TWO HAVEN'T MET, BUT THIS IS *MARCIA.*

SLOWLY SHE LEARNED TO JUDGE FOR HERSELF.

TERRY, IF I'M INTERRUPTING SOMETHING *IMPORTANT...*

NO, NO, YOU'RE *SUPPOSED* TO BE HERE, HONEY. I'M SO SORRY. TIME SLIPPED BY.

SO THIS IS *DONNA.* TERRY, YOU DIDN'T TELL ME SHE WAS SO... *YOUNG.*

YOUNG ENOUGH *NOT* TO HAVE DEVELOPED A *SARCASTIC* STREAK.

WE STILL HAVE JENNY'S *SCHOOL* TO DISCUSS, TERRY.

YOU *DO* FEEL THAT'S IMPORTANT, DON'T YOU?

I MEAN, YOU HARDLY SPEND ANY *TIME* WITH HER IN THE FIRST PLACE.

PLEASE, MARCIA, DO WE HAVE TO DISCUSS THIS *NOW?*

TERRY, IT'S OBVIOUS I'M *INTERRUPTING...*

NO, DONNA. STAY, PLEASE.

I'D RATHER *NOT,* HONEY.

I'M SORRY ABOUT THIS, DONNA. SHE JUST **WOULDN'T LEAVE.**

I **UNDERSTAND.** BELIEVE ME.

LOOK. NO HARD FEELINGS. WE CAN MAKE IT **ANOTHER** DAY.

DADDY, DADDY, YOU GOTTA SEE WHAT I **DID.**

IT'S JUST **GREAT.** YOU'LL LOVE IT.

IT'S **YOU,** DADDY, AND I--

WHO'S **THAT,** DADDY?

SHE'S **DONNA.** SHE'S MY, UHH...

SHE'S DADDY'S **FRIEND,** JENNIFER.

NOW, TERRY, DO I HAVE YOUR **ATTENTION?**

GO RIGHT AHEAD, MRS. **LONG.** I'M **LEAVING.**

I'LL CALL YOU **TOMORROW.**

DAMN.

LONG ISLAND CITY: WHERE THE CITY'S TRAINS GO TO SLEEP. HERE, IN THIS SEEMINGLY ENDLESS SUBWAY GRAVEYARD, A FUTILE ATTEMPT IS MADE TO REPAIR A TRANSPORTATION SYSTEM THAT WAS BUILT AT THE DAWN OF THE TWENTIETH CENTURY.

BUT, WITH BUDGET CUTBACKS, MAINTENANCE CREWS HAVE LONG SINCE VANISHED.

NOW THE ONLY ONES HERE ARE THE VERMIN. THE FOUR LEGGED...

...AND THE **TWO-**LEGGED KIND AS WELL.

20

27

TERRA WAS CORRECT. SHE WAS *EXPECTED* BACK HERE.

I *KNOW* YOU. YOU'RE FROM THE TITANS.

TELL US WHERE YOU HOLD HER *PARENTS.*

TELL US *NOW!*

GET *BACK*, LADY. I'M NOT *TALKING.*

YOU DON'T *HAVE* TO TALK.

NOT WHEN I CAN *REACH* INTO YOUR VERY SOUL AND *TAKE* WHAT I NEED.

SOMETHING IS *WRONG.* THIS MAN KNOWS *NOTHING* OF TERRA'S PARENTS.

ONE OF YOU WILL BE *GLAD* TO TALK.

HE'S PROBABLY JUST *HIRED HELP*, RAVEN. DON'T WORRY. SOMEHOW WE'LL FIND OUT WHAT WE WANT.

RIGHT, BOYS?

NO WAY, SPEED-BOY. WE HAVE OUR JOB AND WE'RE *DOING* IT.

ONE MOVE AND I SWEAR HER PARENTS WILL *DIE.*

NOW DON'T YOU REALLY FEEL LIKE A *JERK?*

HEY, GUYS-- I THINK I'VE *GOT* THE *LEADER* HERE.

HE'S THE ONE WHOSE *I.Q.* TOPS *75.*

BONK

HE RUNS NOW, SEEMINGLY FRIGHTENED. RUNS PAST RAILROAD CARS, HOPING AGAINST HOPE THE TITANS WON'T FOLLOW.

6954

NATURALLY, HE'S WRONG.

LAST *STOP*, MUSCLE-HEAD. THIS IS AS FAR AS YOU *GO.*

CLUNK

OVER HERE. I *GOT* HIM.

21

MAKE HIM TELL WHERE MY *PARENTS* ARE.

IF *YOU* DON'T, I *WILL.*

BE *CALM,* TERRA, WE WILL LEARN THE TRUTH.

YEAH. *LISSEN* TO THE WITCH, SHRIMP. MUSH-FOR-BRAINS HERE'S GONNA TALK.

RIGHT?

I WANT MY *PARENTS.* WHERE *ARE* THEY? *TELL ME!*

TH-THEY'RE *DEAD...THEY'VE BEEN* DEAD ALL ALONG.

THEY DIED BEFORE THEY WERE EVEN TAKEN OUT OF THEIR *COUNTRY.*

WE'VE JUST BEEN *USING* YOU.

NOW... *GASP...* LET GO... *LET GO!*

NO! YOU'RE LYING. THEY *CAN'T* BE DEAD!

I'VE BEEN *SEARCHING* FOR THEM. I KNOW THEY'RE *ALIVE.*

YOU'RE LYING!

AND YOU'LL *PAY* FOR IT!

SHE'S CREATING AN *EARTHQUAKE.*

DIDN'T KNOW SHE WAS *THIS* POWERFUL.

IT'S OKAY. I'LL *STOP* HER. I CAN DO IT.

22

29

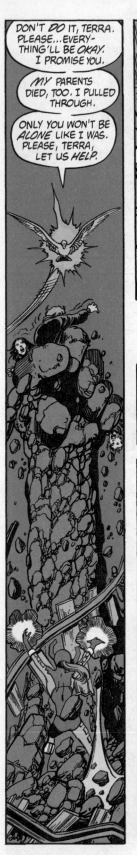

DON'T *DO* IT, TERRA. PLEASE...EVERY-THING'LL BE *OKAY*. I PROMISE YOU.

MY PARENTS DIED, TOO. I PULLED THROUGH.

ONLY YOU WON'T BE *ALONE* LIKE I WAS. PLEASE, TERRA, LET US *HELP*.

NO! I WANT TO *KILL* THIS FILTH. MY PARENTS *CAN'T* BE DEAD.

THEY'RE THE ONLY REASONS I'VE KEPT *GOING*.

THEY'RE THE ONLY ONES WHO EVER *MATTERED* TO ME.

TRUST US, TERRA. DON'T *KILL* THEM. PLEASE... DON'T.

OH, GOD, GAR-- I DON'T KNOW WHAT TO *DO* ANY MORE.

I...FEEL SO ALONE.

YOU DON'T *HAVE* TO BE, TERRA. *I'M* HERE.

WE WILL *HELP* YOU IF THAT IS WHAT YOU TRULY WANT.

MAYBE YOU'RE *RIGHT*. MAYBE I NEED TIME TO THINK.

WHAT DO *YOU* THINK, VIC?

DUNNO. JUST DON'T KNOW.

SOMETHING...BOTHERS ME, BUT I DON'T KNOW WHAT IT IS.

THE GIRL MUST BE FRIGHTENED. SHE SAYS SHE FEELS *ALONE*.

YET WHY DO I SENSE SOMETHING...

...ELSE?

WHY?

23

THE NEW TEEN
TITANS
60¢
U.K.25p
CAN. 75¢
NO. 29
MAR.
APPROVED BY THE COMICS CODE AUTHORITY
SPEEDY
IS BACK...
BUT SO IS THE
BROTHERHOOD
OF EVIL!

FIRST BLOOD!

DEEP BENEATH A TEMPLE IN BUZZARD'S BAY, MASSACHUSETTS...

HIS BODY TENSES, ENJOYING THE MIRACULOUS STRENGTH WHICH FLOWS THROUGH HIM NOW. EACH MUSCLE RIPPLES WITH ENERGY AS HE RENEWS HIS SOLEMN VOW.

ONCE MORE HE IS INVIGORATED, HIS BODY AND SOUL ARE ONE. SOON, HE THINKS, HE MUST RETURN TO HIS NATIVE ZANDIA...THE COMPLETE CEREMONY OF RECLAMATION IS ALMOST AT HAND...

HOWEVER, FOR THE MOMENT, HE IS QUIET, CONTEMPLATIVE, AND HE USES THIS UNEXPECTED PEACE TO PRAY. BUT...

BROTHER BLOOD! I HAVE TO *SPEAK* TO YOU!

MOTHER MAYHEM, YOU KNOW MY RULE AGAINST INTERRUPTING MY *MEDITATION.*

I *DO*-- AND I WOULD NEVER DISTURB YOU WITHOUT GOOD *REASON.*

THE *BROTHERHOOD OF EVIL* HAS LEFT ZANDIA. THEY'RE COMING HERE TO AMERICA-- OBVIOUSLY FOR *YOU!*

I AM *AWARE* OF THEIR DEPARTURE, AND I AM AWARE OF THEIR TRUE *DESTINATION.*

NOTHING OCCURS IN MY HOMELAND WITHOUT MY KNOWLEDGE.

BUT I HAVE ALREADY TAKEN *PRECAUTIONS,* THANK YOU. NOW PLEASE *LEAVE* ME.

BUT THERE'S MORE THAT YOU MAY NOT BE FULLY AWARE OF, SIRE. OUR *TEMPLES* WERE DEFILED.

OUR ACOLYTES TORTURED AND THEN *SLAIN.*

THE *BRAIN* AND HIS *BROTHERHOOD* ARE *TREACHEROUS.* THEY *FRIGHTEN* ME.

THEN I WILL COMFORT YOU LATER IN MY CHAMBERS, AND ONCE AGAIN YOU WILL LEARN WHY *BROTHER BLOOD* FEARS NO MAN, BEAST OR THING.

BUT FIRST, SPREAD THE WORD TO ALL MY BELIEVERS. INSTRUCT THEM TO ATTEND MY *SERMON* TONIGHT.

I SENSE A TIME OF GREAT *URGENCY* BEFALLING US. I WANT ALL WHO WORSHIP ME *PREPARED.*

2

"TELL THEM, TOO, THAT THEIR BROTHERS AND SISTERS WHO *DIED* DEFENDING MY CHURCH SHALL BE *AVENGED.*

"THE TEMPLE OF BROTHER BLOOD MAY *NEVER* BE DEFILED.

"AND NONE SHALL EVER *PUNISH* MY BELIEVERS, SAVE BROTHER BLOOD HIMSELF.

"GO NOW. SPREAD MY WORD QUICKLY AND THEN RETURN THAT I MAY SOOTHE YOUR DEEPEST FEARS AS ONLY *I* CAN."

ZANDIA: BROTHER BLOOD'S CHURCH FADES BENEATH THE SPEEDING JET AS IT LIFTS FROM THE WAR-TORN AIRPORT, RISING HIGH INTO THE DARK, ACRID SKIES.

THE STENCH OF DEATH FILLS ITS HULL, NOT WITH REMORSE, BUT WITH JOY...

YOU HAVE DONE *WELL,* MY BROTHERHOOD. ZE BRAIN IS *PLEASED.*

THEN YOU WILL BE *ECSTATIC* WHEN WE RETURN FROM AMERICA, OUR MISSION *COMPLETE.*

INDEED, PHOBIA. ZHAT I SHALL.

34

BUT REMEMBER, ZE ONE WE SEEK WILL BE WELL-GUARDED. THEY WILL FIGHT TO ZE DEATH TO PREVENT HER ABDUCTION.

ACH! DEN VE VILL KILL DEM ALL, BRAIN.

OUI, MONSIEUR PLASMUS, ZE LOVELY ZEY CALL RAVEN WILL BE OURS!

BUT I WORRY, WARP. REMEMBER, WE MET THESE TITANS ONCE BEFORE. THEY ARE POWERFUL.

ZE BROTHERHOOD SHALL STILL SLAY THEM. DO NOT WORRY SO, MONSIEUR HOUNGAN.

NON, MONSIEUR WARP, HOUNGAN IS CORRECT. DO NOT BELITTLE OUR ENEMY. ZEY ARE STRONG.

FOR ALMOST AN HOUR THE JET THUNDERS ACROSS THE ATLANTIC ON A STEADY COURSE. THEN, SUDDENLY...

MEIN GOTT! DER PLANE -- VAT IS HAPPENING?

BUT THEY WILL NOT STOP US! GO AND BRING ZIS RAVEN TO ME.

WE'RE PLUNGING TOWARD THE OCEAN -- GOING TO CRASH!

DER PILOT, HE DOES THIS. DERE IS NO MALFUNCTION WIT DIS JET.

BEFORE I BECAME DIS CREATURE, I VAS A PILOT. I KNOW DESE JETS--

-- HE IS DELIBERATELY DESTROYING US!

DID YOU TINK DIS FLIMSY STEEL DOOR VOULD KEEP ME AVAY FROM YOU?

SCHWEIN! DID YOU TINK VE VOULD NOT STOP YOU?

VELL, YOU ARE WRONG, SCHWEIN! YOU VILL PAY FOR THIS!

35

PLASMUS' BURNING HAND GRABS THE PILOT, PULLING HIM BACK...

YET, THE PILOT SAYS NOTHING AS HIS CLOTHING BEGINS TO BURN.

THERE IS NO CRY OR PLEA AS HIS FLESH BEGINS TO SIZZLE...

...AND-- MELT?

LIEBER GOTT! HE'S A-- ROBOT!

BROTHER BLOOD IS BEHIND THIS.

I VANT HIM--MORE DAN EVER.

VE MUST NOT DIE!

THEN HURRY, YOU FOOLS! LOOK!

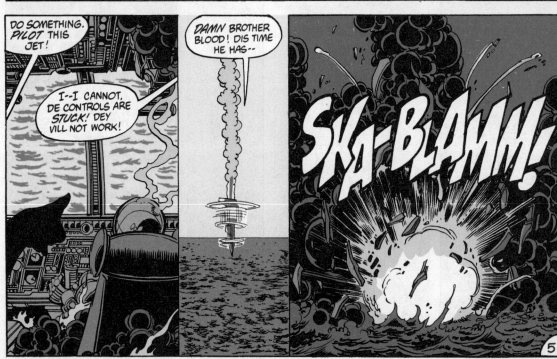

DO SOMETHING. PILOT THIS JET!

I--I CANNOT. DE CONTROLS ARE STUCK! DEY VILL NOT WORK!

DAMN BROTHER BLOOD! DIS TIME HE HAS--

SKA-BLAMM!

5

NEW YORK'S EAST RIVER... AND THE SMALL ISLAND UPON WHICH *TITANS'* TOWER STANDS.

INSIDE THIS IMPOSING EDIFICE LIVE THE GREATEST HEROES IN NEW YORK CITY.

HE IS ONE OF THEM. HIS NAME IS *DICK GRAYSON*, AND HE IS THE UN-CHALLENGED LEADER OF THE TEEN TITANS.

TODAY, DICK GRAYSON IS ANGRY...

...AND ANGRY, HE TAKES OUT HIS FRUSTRATIONS IN EXERCISE.

HIS MUSCLES STRAIN AND PULL. THE PAST HOUR HAS BEEN GRUEL-ING, YET HE SHOWS NO SIGNS OF FATIGUE.

DICK GRAYSON IS ANGRY WITH HIMSELF, AND SO HE CONTINUES TO *PUNISH* HIMSELF LONG AFTER A SANER MAN WOULD HAVE STOPPED.

6

YOU'RE DETERMINED TO *HURT* YOURSELF, AREN'T YOU?

I'M DOING JUST *FINE,* DONNA. NO *PROBLEMS.*

PHYSICALLY YOU'RE RIGHT. *MENTALLY,* YOU'RE *TORTURING* YOURSELF TO ACHIEVE SOME *IDEAL* THAT'S IMPOSSIBLE TO REACH.

YOU'LL NEVER BE *THE BATMAN.* DICK, WANT TO TALK?

NOTHING TO TALK *ABOUT.*

I'M FINE. LET ME BE.

DICK, THERE'S ABSOLUTELY NO ONE I'M *CLOSER* TO IN THE TITANS THAN YOU. I CAN'T LET THIS GO.

I CARE TOO MUCH. YOU'RE DRIVING YOURSELF *INSANE.*

YOU'RE TRYING TO DO IT ALL, BUT YOU *CAN'T.* I HATE TO LET YOU IN ON THIS, PAL--

--BUT YOU'RE ONLY *HUMAN.* YOU'VE GOT TO *STOP.* WORKING WITH *US.* WORKING *ALONE.* WITH *THE BATMAN.* GOING TO SCHOOL...

YOU'VE SET YOUR-SELF AN IMPOSSIBLE *CHALLENGE.*

DONNA, I APPRECIATE YOUR CONCERN, BUT YOU'RE *WRONG.* I CAN DO THIS.

I *HAVE* TO.

OKAY, I WON'T PUSH... NOT *TODAY.* JUST TAKE CARE OF YOURSELF. AND TALK WHEN YOU CAN.

SURE. TAKE CARE. I'LL *SEE* YOU.

7

JUST WISH I KNEW *WHY* DICK IS PUSHING HIM-SELF. IT'S DRIVING *KORY* UP THE WALL.

POOR KID KEEPS THINKING IT'S SOME-THING *SHE* DID.

GREAT! I'M WORRYING ABOUT EVERYONE ELSE WHEN I'VE GOT MY *OWN* PROBLEMS.

I WAS AN ABSOLUTE *IDIOT* LAST NIGHT WITH TERRY.

BUT I FELT SO *UNCOM-FORTABLE* SEEING HIM AND HIS WIFE... NO, IT'S NOT HIS *EX.* SHE DOESN'T BOTHER ME. IT WAS HIS *DAUGHTER.* SHE'S THE ONE. I SAW A *FAMILY* IN HER...

NO MATTER WHAT'S *HAPPENED* BETWEEN HER PARENTS, SHE WILL ALWAYS *KNOW* WHO THEY ARE.

WHICH IS MORE THAN I DO ABOUT *MINE.*

THE ROOM IS SMALL, BUT LARGE ENOUGH FOR RAVEN'S NEEDS. THE AIR IS SCENTED WITH JASMINE, FAR TOO SWEET FOR WALLY WEST, BUT HE SAYS NOTHING.

WALLACE, I CANNOT DO YOUR SCHOOL WORK *FOR YOU...*

FORGET SCHOOL. I NEED TO GET *US* FIGURED OUT.

THERE CAN BE NO *"US."* I LIKE YOU... DEEPLY. BUT WHAT I AM *PRE-CLUDES* MY LOVING YOU.

I DARE NOT ALLOW MYSELF THAT EMOTION.

JUST OUTSIDE THE CLOSED DOOR...

SOMETIMES I FEEL I'M DENYING *MY* OWN EMOTIONS, RAVEN. NOT KNOW-ING WHO I AM *DOES* THAT TO ME.

SOMETIMES I DON'T FEEL LIKE I BELONG. I SHOULDN'T. BUT I *DO.*

I KNOW THAT, RAVEN, BUT I *LOVE* YOU.

BUT *I* CANNOT LOVE *YOU.* IF I FAIL TO REIGN IN MY EMOTIONS, THAT PART OF ME WHICH IS MY FATHER *TRIGON* CAN BURST FREE.

I'VE GOT TO DO SOMETHING ...*SOON.* I CAN'T KEEP *DENYING* MY HERITAGE.

I'VE GOT TO *KNOW* WHAT I TRULY AM.

YOU CANNOT UNDERSTAND THE *PAIN* I LIVE WITH, TRYING TO *CONTROL* MY DARKER SIDE.

YOU ASK FOR ADVICE? *LEAVE* THE TITANS! RETURN TO SCHOOL. *FORGET ME.*

IF YOU STAY, I SWEAR I SHALL BE THE *DEATH* OF YOU!

8

A SMALL ISLAND IN THE MID-ATLANTIC...

GULF-STREAM WATERS WARM THIS VEST-POCKET ISLE, MAKING IT A VERITABLE *PARADISE*...

WHICH IS EXACTLY THE THOUGHT OF THESE FOUR HAGGARD TRAVELERS...

WH-WHERE ARE WE?

VHERE HAF YOU *TELEPORTED* US, WARP?

I AM NOT SURE, MON AMI... I HAD TO WARP US OFF THAT PLUNGING JET TOO QUICKLY TO *CHOOSE* MY DESTINATION.

ARE YOU STRONG ENOUGH TO TELEPORT US TO *AMERICA?*

NON... GIVE ME A MOMENT. TO CARRY ALL *FOUR* OF US IS A TERRIBLE *STRAIN.*

I CANNOT *WAIT,* HERR WARP. MY ANGER TOWARD BROTHER BLOOD GROWS WITH EVERY SECOND.

ALRIGHT, PLASMUS-- BUT WE MUST MAKE ZIS VOYAGE IN *STAGES...*

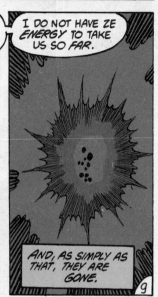

I DO NOT HAVE ZE *ENERGY* TO TAKE US SO *FAR.*

AND, AS SIMPLY AS THAT, THEY ARE GONE.

9

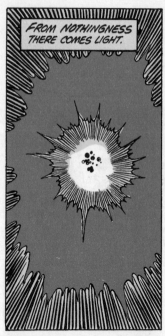

FROM NOTHINGNESS THERE COMES LIGHT.

AND FROM THE LIGHT APPEARS THE BROTHERHOOD OF EVIL...

NOW *VHERE* ARE WE, HERR WARP?

NOT FAR FROM OUR GOAL, MON AMI. BUT PLEASE, LET ME REST.

TO USE MY POWERS SO BROADLY WEAKENS ME.

THEN VE VAIT. BUT DO NOT *DELAY.* DER FORCES WHICH CHURN WITHIN ME... DEMAND I SLAY OUR ENEMY.

YOU WILL GET YOUR *CHANCE,* MON AMI-- AFTER WE ABDUCT THIS RAVEN... NOT BEFORE.

MINUTES PASS, THEN...

B WHAT?

LASERS!?!

PHOBIA SNAPS TO ATTENTION, HER HEAD CRANING UPWARD, GAZING AT THE JET-AND-CRIMSON FIGURES WHO SLIDE IN ON MINI-FLYERS.

THESE ARE BROTHER BLOOD'S *MISSIONARIES,* SET TO CARRY OUT THE ORDERS OF *EXCOMMUNICATION.*

BUT...

MY POOR, DELUDED FRIENDS, *WE* ARE NOT YOUR ENEMY. GAZE INTO THE *EYES* OF PHOBIA--

--AND YOU WILL *LEARN* WHO YOU MUST TRULY FEAR.

11

NEW YORK CITY. WINTRY DAYS TAKE HOLD AS THE LONG INDIAN SUMMER FINALLY FADES...

AND THIS GIRL *SHIVERS* WHILE GAZING LONGINGLY AT THE FAMILIAR SITE HALFWAY ACROSS THE EAST RIVER.

THESE PAST MONTHS SHE HAS BEEN SO *FRIGHTENED,* BUT NOW SHE KNOWS WHAT MUST BE DONE.

AND, MARVELLING AT THE *CONTROL* SHE HAS GAINED IN SO SHORT A TIME, SHE RISES SEVERAL *FEET* INTO THE AIR...

...*GLIDING* QUICKLY TOWARD HER DESTINATION.

WHILE WITHIN...

HIYA, BEAUTIFUL. HOW'S IT GOING?

EVERYTHING IS JUST *FINE,* ROY. ARE YOU ENJOYING YOUR VISIT HERE?

WITH GIRLS LIKE *YOU* AROUND, WHO WOULDN'T? WANNA TAKE IN A FLICK?

SOMETHING WRONG, *STARFIRE?* IS IT *DICK?*

I'M *SORRY.* I DIDN'T KNOW I WAS SO OBVIOUS.

ROY, YOU'VE *KNOWN* HIM A LONG TIME. WHY HAS HE BECOME SO MOODY?

IS HE *ANGRY* WITH ME?

YOU KNOW, SOMETIMES I BECOME SO *CONFUSED.* I STILL DON'T UNDERSTAND YOU EARTHLINGS.

MY GORGEOUS, BEAUTIFUL FRIEND, I *AM* AN EARTHLING, AS YOU SO SWEETLY PUT IT--

--AND EVEN *I* DON'T UNDERSTAND OUR POOR RICHARD GRAYSON.

WHY DON'T YOU *FORGET* ABOUT HIM? *I* COULD CERTAINLY CHEER UP THAT DOUR FACE.

12

YOU DON'T TAKE *LONG*, DO YOU, ROY?

YOU JUST *MOVE* IN AND-- *WHAM!*

DICK? WE WERE JUST *TALKING* ABOUT YOU.

SURE YOU WERE, ROY. I *HEARD.*

STAY AWAY FROM KORY. SHE'S NOT *YOURS.*

OH, I'M REALLY SORRY. I DIDN'T KNOW YOU HAD A *BILL OF SALE.*

ROY, PLEASE...

OKAY, FOR *YOU* I WON'T CONTINUE THIS. BUT CAN I HAVE A *KISS* FIRST... TO REMEMBER OUR PRECIOUS *SECONDS* TOGETHER?

YOU CAN HAVE THIS *SPOON.* MAKE YOUR OWN SOUP.

WHO WAS THAT *LADLE* I SAW YOU WITH LAST NIGHT? THAT WAS NO LADLE, THAT WAS MY *KNIFE!*

"THAT WAS NO LADLE"? WHAT DOES HE *MEAN* BY THAT?

FORGET HIM.

DICK, WE WERE JUST *TALKING*, YOU DIDN'T HAVE TO GET SO *ANGRY!*

HEY, BEAUTIFUL. *HANG* IN THERE.

AND IF THE BIG *G* DOESN'T WISE UP. I'LL STILL BE HERE.

DICK, THAT WAS REALLY *UNCALLED* FOR.

LOOK, I'M ON MY WAY TO SEE ADRIAN CHASE. IT SEEMS *BETHANY SNOW* JUST CALLED HIM ABOUT BROTHER BLOOD.

ARE YOU INTERESTED IN COMING WITH ME, OR WOULD YOU RATHER *STAY* HERE?

OF COURSE I *WANT* TO COME WITH YOU, BUT--

GOOD! THEN LET'S GO.

13

BUZZARD'S BAY, MASSACHUSETTS...

BROTHER BLOOD, SISTER BETHANY IS HERE.

CHASE AND THE TITANS HAVE AN *APPOINTMENT* WITH ME, FOR LATER.

EXCELLENT, SISTER BETHANY. DO THIS TASK WELL AND YOU WILL BE AMPLY *REWARDED.*

I WILL, M'LORD. I'VE *MEMORIZED* ALL THE INFORMATION. THEY WILL BELIEVE ME.

MAKE *CERTAIN* THEY DO. I NEED ZANDIA'S *AGREEMENT* WITH THE UNITED STATES RATIFIED, AND YOU ARE THE *KEY* TO THAT SUCCESS.

SISTER BETHANY, DO *NOT* FAIL ME.

SOMEWHERE IN THE ATLANTIC LIE THE REMAINS OF BROTHER BLOOD'S MISSIONARIES. THEIR *DEATHS* WERE SWIFT, AND FOR SOME--PAINLESS.

WHILE, ACROSS THE OCEAN, THEIR MASTER *SMILES;* ALL GOES WELL.

ABOVE THIS ISLE DE MORTE...

HOW KIND OF BLOOD TO *SUPPLY* US WITH THESE FLIERS. IT MAKES MY WORK THAT MUCH EASIER, NON?

EASIER, WARP-- BUT NOT *FASTER.*

THE BRAIN WILL NOT BE *PLEASED* WITH THIS DELAY.

C'EST LA *GUERRE,* EH?

I WORK *WITH* ZE BRAIN, NOT *FOR* HIM.

AH, MONSIEUR HOUNGAN--AND *YOU?*

I WORK *FOR* HIM, MONSIEUR WARP. I OWE HIM BOTH *MY LIFE* AND MY POWER TO CONTROL THESE *COMPUTERIZED FETISHES.*

14

TITANS TOWER...

...I'M NOT SAYING I DON'T *TRUST* YOU, TERRA-- BUT WHY DIDN'T YOU USE YOUR *EARTH-SHIFTING* POWERS TO *STOMP* THOSE TERRORISTS?

CAN THE *QUESTIONS*, BOZO. MIND YOUR OWN BUSINESS.

HI, GUYS. HOW'S IT GOING?

YOU *SHUT UP* TOO, ARCHER.

YEAH, I GUESS IT WILL BE A *NICE* DAY IF IT DOESN'T RAIN.

LOOK, I JUST LEARNED MY *PARENTS* ARE DEAD. CAN'T YOU *LEAVE ME ALONE?*

THAT'S *ANOTHER* THING. IF YOUR DAD WAS A *KING*, WHY DIDN'T YOU HEAR ANY *NEWS* OF HIS DEATH?

THOSE TERRORISTS DIDN'T EXACTLY *LOCK* YOU AWAY.

LET'S GET THIS *STRAIGHT*, GREENIE. I DON'T ANSWER TO YOU. BUG OFF! DON'T BOTHER ME! *SCRAM!*

CALM DOWN, TERRA. WE TITANS DON'T *ARGUE* AMONG OURSELVES LIKE THIS. WE WORK *TOGETHER.*

NOW ISN'T THAT JUST *SWEETNESS AND LIGHT?*

FIRST OFF, I'M *NOT* A TITAN.

SECOND, I'M NOT *BECOMING* ONE.

AND THIRD-- BUTT OUT!

OOOF!

SK-K

TERRA? WAIT A SECOND. COME *BACK* HERE!

LOGAN?

NOT NOW, VIC, I'M IN A *RUSH.*

TERRA!?!

15

VICTOR, MY FRIEND, I THINK *REFORMING* TERRA'S BECOME LOGAN'S PERSONAL CRUSADE.

IF THAT'S THE CASE, HARPER, THEN I THINK HE'S *BITTEN OFF* EVEN MORE THAN HIS OVER-SIZED MOUTH *CAN* CHEW.

I GOT SOME WORK TO DO UP IN THE MACHINE SHOP. WANNA *HELP?*

NAH! STILL HAVEN'T HAD *LUNCH.*

SUIT YOURSELF.

WHILE, IN ANOTHER ROOM...

NO USE. THIS STUFF PUTS ME *TO SLEEP.* I THOUGHT *CONRAD* WAS SUPPOSED TO BE BRILLIANT.

THE GUY USES FOUR THOUSAND WORDS WHEN *TWO* WOULD DO.

NEVER BEEN MUCH OF A READER ANY-WAY--EH? PICKING UP *VIBRATIONS...* EMERGENCY ALARM'S ABOUT TO RING.

EEEEEEEEEEEEEEEEEEEEEEEEEEEEEE

WHAT'S THAT?

SOUNDS LIKE ME TRYING TO *SING.*

TROUBLE! SOMEONE *UNAUTHORIZED* LANDED ON THE ISLAND.

NO, VICTOR...IT IS *NOT* TROUBLE.

"I SENSE...A FRIEND."

HI, WALLY.

FRANCES KANE? I DON'T BELIEVE IT.

Y-YOU'RE *FLOATING?* BUT I THOUGHT YOU *LOST* YOUR POWERS.

I'M SO *HAPPY* TO SEE YOU, WALLY. FOR A WHILE I DIDN'T THINK I'D HAVE THE *NERVE* TO COME BACK HERE--AFTER WHAT HAPPENED.

I THOUGHT EVERY-THING WAS GOING TO *CHANGE.* BUT THEN THE *MAG-NETIC POWERS* CAME BACK... AND I GOT SO *SCARED* AGAIN...

I *HAD* TO SEE.

16

AND, MERE MOMENTS LATER...

WELL, WELL, I *KNEW* THERE WAS A REASON I HUNG AROUND.

MY NAME'S *SPEEDY*, BUT THAT'S NOT INDICATIVE OF *EVERYTHING* I DO.

LONG TIME, FRAN. HOW'S THINGS?

WHAT IS *WRONG*, FRANCES? I SENSE *CONCERN*.

I AM, RAVEN. SOMETHING'S *WRONG*.

LISTEN, IT'S *COLD* OUT HERE. LET'S GO INSIDE. I'LL MAKE SOME *HOT CHOCOLATE*.

I DON'T GET IT. SO FAR I'VE *STRUCK OUT* WITH EVERYONE BUT TERRA--

--AND I *NEVER* MAKE A PLAY FOR GIRLS WHOSE *AGE* IS SMALLER THAN MY STRING SIZE!

DON'T *WORRY* ABOUT IT, ARCHER. FRANCES AN' WALLY GO WAY BACK.

SO? THAT'S *NEVER* STOPPED ME BEFORE.

I MUST BE *LOSING* THE OL' ROY HARPER CHARM.

LEMME KNOW HOW THINGS WORK OUT. SEEYA LATER, MAN.

MEANWHILE, IN MANHATTAN...

TRUST US WHEN WE SAY, THAT SOON WILL *CHANGE*.

THANK YOU, MRS. CHASE.

PLEASE, CALL ME DORIS.

YOUR CHILDREN ARE *BEAUTIFUL*, DORIS. I LOVE CHILDREN. DON'T YOU, ROBIN?

THEY'RE SO *INNOCENT*, SO FULL OF LIFE.

STARFIRE, WE'RE HERE ON *BUSINESS*.

ADRIAN SAID HE'D BE RIGHT OUT. YOU CAN--UH--*WAIT* FOR HIM.

I KNOW, BUT WE CAN STILL *ENJOY* SOME PLEASURES.

HYDRAULIC LEGS PROPEL CYBORG TOWARD MANHATTAN. AT THE MOMENT VICTOR STONE IS HAPPY.

IT IS TIME TO MOVE ON, ROY HARPER THINKS, POURING HIMSELF THE LAST OF THE TOMATO-RICE SOUP. THE TRIP WAS SUCCESSFUL, BUT...

HE HEARS THE QUIET POP OF RUSHING AIR BEHIND HIM JUST MOMENTS BEFORE THE LIGHT EXPLODES.

THEN...

I TOLD YOU I WAS STRONG ENOUGH TO WARP THE LAST MILES HERE.

WHILE...

WALLACE, I SENSE--THE BROTHERHOOD? THEY ARE IN THE KITCHEN.

WHO?

HE'S STILL COMING AT ME. I HAVE NO CHOICE--I HAVE TO SHOOT.

NOT THAT I THINK IT WILL STOP HIM.

C'MON, YOU DON'T REALLY WANNA FIGHT ME, DO YOU?

NO, SCHWEIN-- I VANT TO KILL YOU.

I VANT TO REDUCE YOUR MISERABLE FLESH TO ITS BASIC PROTOPLASMIC SLIME!

DIS IS TITANS' TOWER? VHERE ARE THE TITANS? TELL ME!

HOO BOY, SOMETHING TELLS ME YOU'RE NOT FRIENDS DROPPING IN.

STAND BACK, JELLO-FACE. AND THAT GOES FOR THE REST OF YOU.

OH, GOD-- JUST WHAT WE DIDN'T NEED. HALF THE TEAM'S OUT.

FRAN, YOU STAY HERE. C'MON, RAVEN-- LET'S GO.

WELL, UGLY, YOU CAN'T GET EVERYTHING YOU WANT.

WATCH THESE GUYS. THEY'RE DANGEROUS.

THAT YOU DIDN'T HAVE TO TELL ME.

19

KID FLASH? *GOOD!* I CAME PREPARED. MY *FETISH* IS ALREADY PROGRAMMED TO YOUR CELL TYPE.

A SINGLE TOUCH WITH MY *COMPUTERIZED NEEDLE* AND SCIENCE AND SORCERY WORK AS ONE.

MY LEG!!

WITHOUT TOUCHING HIM, THE NEEDLE *CUTS* THROUGH FLESH AND MUSCLE, RIPPING THROUGH TENDON AND BONE.

KID FLASH STUMBLES IN PAIN. HE FALLS AND *STAYS DOWN.*

THERE IS RAVEN...I WILL SEND HER TO OUR *WAITING STATION.* SHE WILL *NOT* BE ABLE TO ESCAPE.

NO!

THE SOMBER EMPATH *SENSES* THE TRAP EVEN BEFORE IT IS SPRUNG.

AND EVEN AS HER BODY FALLS THROUGH THE SPATIAL WARP, HER *SOUL SELF* SLIPS FREE.

WHY HAVE YOU *DONE* THIS TO ME?

AND WHERE HAVE YOU SENT MY *CORPOREAL BODY?* SPEAK TO ME? TELL ME!

RAVEN!

WARP IS NOT YOUR FOE. *LOOK* AROUND YOU. SEE YOUR *WORST FEAR* COME ALIVE.

HE IS HERE, NOW!

HE WILL *DESTROY* YOU, DESTROY EVERYTHING YOU HOLD DEAR.

N-NO!

THERE? BUT THAT IS WAL--

TRIGON?

AZAR GUIDE ME! MY FATHER HAS SLAIN WALLACE!

NO, RAVEN-- IT'S ME. MY GOD-- *STOP,* RAVEN!

20

51

WHATEVER YOU'VE DONE TO HER-- *STOP IT!*

FOR GOD'S SAKE, RAVEN--CAN YOU *HEAR ME?* STOP!

BUT RAVEN HEARS NOTHING SAVE THE POUNDING OF HER FEARFUL HEART.

HER SOUL-SELF IS THE PART OF HER WHICH IS TRIGON. NOW THAT SOUL-SELF IS *OUT OF CONTROL.*

I COULDN'T STAY BACK, WALLY. I--

OH, NO--WHAT'S GOING ON HERE?

WALLY?

IT *HURTS...*PLEASE...STOP, RAVEN--YOU'RE KILLING ME.

SO COLD...IT'S *HORRIBLE...* I--I CAN'T TAKE IT.

FRANCES KANE *REACTS* WITHOUT THINKING. ONCE, MANY YEARS AGO, SHE HAD LOVED WALLY WEST...

SHE MAY *STILL* LOVE HIM.

BUT WHATEVER HER FEELINGS, SHE WILL *NOT* SIT BACK AND WATCH HIM DIE.

STOP HER! SHE MUST NOT PREVENT US FROM CON-TROLLING RAVEN.

DO NOT VORRY, PHOBIA. SHE VILL NOT USE DOSE *POWERS* ON THE ONE VE VANT.

DER BRAIN SENT US FOR RAVEN. *NOTHING* VILL STOP US FROM ABDUCTING HER.

AND, IF I MUST *KILL* TO ASSURE OUR GOAL, DEN SO BE IT.

DAT VHICH I AM CRIES OUT FOR BLOOD.

REALLY, PAL, THEN TRY *MINE*--IF YOU'RE MAN ENOUGH.

YOU *ARE* A MAN BENEATH ALL THAT MUCK, AREN'T YOU?

21

BUT...

NO!

WHAT HAVE I DONE?

THE SOUL-SELF VANISHES. THEN...

HEY, PAL, HOW ARE --

SH-SHE WAS SO *COLD*...LIKE *DEATH*...LIKE THE *DYING*...

SHE--SHE WANTS TO *KILL* ME. THE HATE...I SAW HER HATE. I COULD *TOUCH* IT.

I SAW HER...GOD, FOR THE *FIRST TIME*-- I SAW HER...

SAW HER...SAW *TRIGON*...MY GOD... HER SOUL...TRIGON ...THEY--THEY'RE LIKE *ONE*...

I--I NEVER KNEW ...SHE-SHE COULD HAVE DESTROYED ME.

I RETRIEVED MY BODY-- WITHOUT THE BROTHERHOOD PRESENT, THEIR *TRAP* COULDN'T HOLD ME.

WALLACE! THANK *AZAR.* I THOUGHT I HAD *SLAIN* YOU.

GET *AWAY* FROM ME, RAVEN. *STAY AWAY!*

YOU WOULD HAVE *KILLED* ME.

WALLACE, PLEASE *UNDERSTAND.* MY SOUL-SELF WAS OUT OF CONTROL. I COULD NOT *CONTAIN* MY DARK SIDE.

IT WAS *NOT* ME.

STAY *AWAY* FROM ME, RAVEN.

JUST *STAY AWAY!*

I--I CANNOT TAKE YOUR *HATE*...I MUST LEAVE...MUST *GO*... MUST *THINK!*

WELL, ROY, HOW DID *YOU* SPEND YOUR WINTER VACATION?

SHE'S GONE, BUT I DON'T THINK SHE *KNEW* WHAT SHE WAS DOING.

SHE KNEW, FRAN-- BELIEVE ME. *SHE KNEW!*

AND MORE-- SHE *ENJOYED* IT!

23

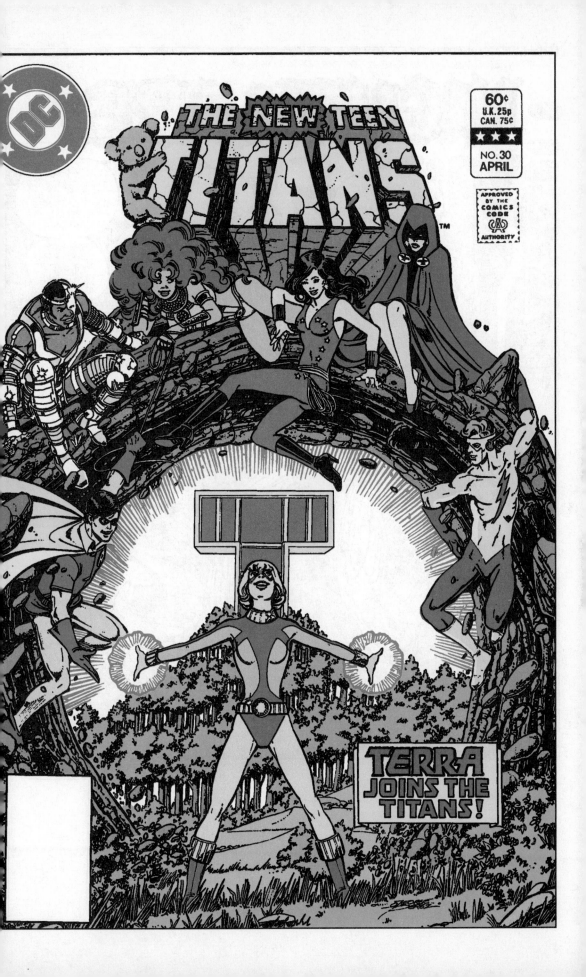

A NEW TEEN TITAN JOINS IN TIME TO BE PART OF A NEW YEAR'S...

NIGHTMARE!

HOLD ON, WALLY. I'M BRINGING A CHAIR FOR YOU *MAGNETICALLY.*

MAYBE I DON'T KNOW RAVEN LIKE *YOU* DO, BUT I STILL DON'T THINK SHE'S *EVIL.*

FRAN'S RIGHT, PAL. YOU TOLD US YOURSELF THAT HER FATHER TRIGON, WAS *PART* OF HER SOUL-SELF.

THE PART SHE FIGHTS TO *SUPPRESS.*

BUT WHEN *PHOBIA* DUG INTO RAVEN'S SUBCONSCIOUS, SHE LEARNED THAT HER GREATEST FEAR WAS *UNLEASHING* HER EVIL SIDE.

RAVEN COULDN'T *HELP* WHAT HAPPENED TO HER.

I-I DON'T CARE. SHE'S *EVIL...* I KNOW THE TRUTH NOW.

H-HOW COULD I HAVE TRIED TO *LOVE* HER?

WALLY, I CAME HERE POSSESSING SUPER-POWERS I DIDN'T *WANT.*

SOMETHING TELLS ME YOU WOULD RATHER FORGET *YOUR* SUPER-HEROICS AS WELL.

WHY DON'T WE BOTH GO BACK TO *BLUE VALLEY*-- PLEASE, WALLY?

LEAVE THE *TITANS?* FRAN, RIGHT NOW THAT SOUNDS SO *TEMPTING...*

LORD, I DON'T KNOW... I NEVER SEEM TO KNOW *WHAT* TO DO.

I HATE TO *SAY* THIS, PAL, BUT FRAN COULD BE *RIGHT.*

YOU'RE ALWAYS SAYING YOU CAN'T PLAY SUPER-HERO WHILE GOING TO *SCHOOL*--

--SO WHY DON'T YOU DO WHAT *I* DO-- GO ON *RESERVE STATUS*... BE A *PART-TIME* TITAN.

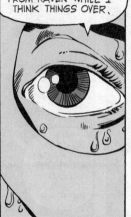

PART-TIME? TH-THAT WOULD KEEP ME AWAY FROM RAVEN WHILE I THINK THINGS OVER.

I-I'VE GOT TO *THINK* ABOUT THIS, REALLY *THINK* ABOUT IT.

2

MY DEAR, PHOBIA HAS NO DESIRE TO *HARM* YOU.

I DO, HOWEVER, WISH TO *WARN* YOU.

IF YOU DO NOT LIKE THIS SUDDEN FEELING OF *SPACE* CRUSHING IN ON YOU--

--STAY OUT OF OUR *WAY*. OR, WHEN *NEXT* WE MEET...

...I MAY NOT SO QUICKLY FREE YOU FROM THE CLUTCHES OF *CLAUSTROPHOBIA*!

JUST IN CASE, I HAD BETTER FIX A LOCK OF THIS ONE'S *HAIR* TO MY FETISH.

WE MAY ONE DAY *NEED* THIS, EH?

D-DON'T... PLEASE DON'T *DO* THAT AGAIN.

WELL, WARP, I HAVE GIVEN YOU RAVEN'S *DOLL*-- HAVE YOU HOMED IN ON HER *LOCATION*?

NOT *PRECISELY*, MONSIEUR, BUT I CAN BRING US *NEAR* HER.

NOW COME, LET US HURRY BEFORE SHE *VANISHES* AGAIN.

THE BROTHERHOOD IS PLEASED. THINGS HAVE GONE *WELL* THUS FAR, AND IF THEY *CONTINUE* THAT WAY, THEY WILL SOON HAVE RAVEN IN THEIR CLUTCHES...

...AND WITH HER, THE SECRET OF BROTHER BLOOD!

WARP EXPLODES WITH LIGHT, TRANSPORTING HIMSELF AND HIS COMRADES ACROSS THE LENGTH OF MANHATTAN...

WALLY? SPEEDY? PLEASE ...SOMEONE... *HELP ME!*

PLEASE!!

4

SEVERAL MILES SOUTH STANDS THE WORLD-FAMOUS *BROOKLYN BRIDGE*, SOLD TO ALL-TOO-MANY UNWARY TOURISTS LOOKING FOR A BIG APPLE *BARGAIN.*

YOU *LIVED* HERE, TARA? EVEN *COCKROACHES* WOULD PICKET A HOLE LIKE THIS.

THIS PLACE ISN'T EVEN FIT FOR *PIGEONS* TO DO YOU-KNOW-WHAT ON.

THIS DUMP'S NATIONAL BIRD IS *THE VULTURE!*

WILL YOU KNOCK OFF THE DUMB *JOKES*, LOGAN? I WAS BEING HELD *PRISONER* HERE, REMEMBER?

THERE AREN'T TOO MANY *TERRORISTS* WHO CAN AFFORD TO HOLE UP AT THE *PLAZA.*

YEAH, THAT'S SOMETHING I WAS *WONDERING* ABOUT. YOU HAD *SUPER-POWERS.* WHY DIDN'T YOU USE 'EM AND *FORCE* THOSE TERRORISTS TO TELL YOU ABOUT YOUR PARENTS?

I DON'T WANT TO *TALK* ABOUT THAT.

HEY, LOGAN, I HAVE NO PLACE TO *GO* NOW. YOU THINK I COULD STAY WITH *YOU* GUYS?

Y'KNOW, BECOME A *TEEN TITAN?* AH... *THERE* IT IS!

BECOME A *TITAN?* I *GUESS* SO. WE HAVEN'T GOT ANY *RULES* ABOUT THAT.

POLITICAL PRISONERS

FREE

PLO

SO WHAT DID YOU *FIND* BACK THERE?

I ORIGINALLY MADE *TWO* COSTUMES TO WEAR AS *TERRA--* BUT I SWORE I'D ONLY WEAR *THIS* ONE WHEN I WAS FINALLY *FREE.*

YEAH, IT STILL *FITS.*

SCREWBALL, TURN AROUND THIS WAY...

5

WELL, HOW ABOUT AN *ANSWER*?

WELL--ah--ACTUALLY, IT'S NOT UP TO *ME*.

I GOTTA CHECK IT OUT WITH THE OTHERS. WE'RE SORTA *EXCLUSIVE*.

SURE, SURE. THEN LET'S PUT ON SOME *WING-SPEED*, WILLYA?

I WANT AN *ANSWER* ON THIS--*FAST*!

WHILE, BELOW...

CHASE, YOU HAVEN'T SAID A *WORD* THE WHOLE TRIP. WHAT'S *WRONG*?

WELL, KID, YOU REMEMBER THAT DRUG-PUSHER, ANTHONY *SCARAPELLI*? FROM THE *RUNAWAY* CASE?

HE JUST *BOUGHT* HIS WAY CLEAR.

SNOW STORM
CABLE NEWS STARRING BETHANY SNOW

THIS IS WHAT *GETS* ME, ROBIN. I HAD SCARAPELLI DOWN *COLD*--BUT NOW HE'S *FREE*.

LOOK, LET'S *FORGET* IT FOR NOW, OKAY? WE'RE AFTER *BROTHER BLOOD*.

YOU DO KNOW THIS IS PROBABLY A *SET-UP*. BETHANY SNOW *WORKS* FOR BLOOD.

TELL ME SOMETHING I *DON'T* KNOW.

YEAH, BLOOD'S *UP* TO SOMETHING... SOMETHING ABOUT THE UPCOMING *CONGRESSIONAL ELECTIONS*.

YOU REALLY THINK SHE'LL *HELP* US?

BEATS *ME*, STARFIRE-- BUT I CAN'T AFFORD TO OVERLOOK ANY OPPORTUNITIES.

BESIDES, I'M *PAID* TO WORK MY EIGHT HOURS.

THOUGH WHY YOU CLOWNS DO THIS FOR *FREE* I'LL NEVER KNOW.

ON THE AIR

STUDIO 11

THE DOOR'S *OPEN*.

THEN LET'S PLAY THE *FLIES* TO BETHANY SNOW'S *SPIDER*. C'MON!

7

WELL, MISS SNOW, WE'RE *HERE.*

WHY DID YOU *CALL US?*

SN ST... BETHA...

SNOW STORM with BETHA...

SNOW...

OH, THANK GOD, I WAS GOING *CRAZY* WAITING FOR YOU.

LOOK, I KNOW YOU THINK I'M *LYING* ABOUT THIS, BUT I'M NOT.

I--I WANT BLOOD *STOPPED.*

OKAY, I *ADMIT* I WORKED FOR HIM. I HELPED HIM SET THE TITANS *UP* THAT'LL *PROVE* I'M BEING STRAIGHT.

ONLY IF YOU'RE WILLING TO GO ON THE *RECORD.*

I AM. *BELIEVE* ME.

WHY THE SUDDEN *CHANGE,* MISS SNOW?

BECAUSE I JUST LEARNED WHAT BROTHER BLOOD IS *REALLY* AFTER.

LOOK, I *BELIEVED* IN HIM. I REALLY DID. I THOUGHT HE WAS OUT TO CREATE A *BETTER* WORLD.

OH, I WASN'T *BLIND* TO HIS DARK SIDE, BUT I BELIEVED HIS ENDS *JUSTIFIED* HIS MEANS.

YOU STILL DON'T BELIEVE ME. THEN LOOK AT *THIS.*

WELL, WELL. BROTHER BLOOD WAS *THOROUGH* WITH HIS RECORDS. CAN WE *KEEP* THESE?

OF COURSE... SHOW THEM TO THE *PRESS.*

THESE PHOTOGRAPHS ARE *PROOF* OF BLOOD'S REIGN OF TORTURE.

8

X'HAL! WHY DIDN'T YOU *TELL* ME HE DID THIS TO YOU?

H-HE COULD HAVE *KILLED* YOU, ROBIN.

HE DIDN'T.

OKAY, SO WE *BUY* YOUR STORY -- FOR *NOW*, WHAT'S BLOOD *UP TO*?

IT'S THE *SPECIAL ELECTIONS* BEING HELD IN THREE STATES NEXT MONTH.

THESE PEOPLE -- THE FIRST TWO ARE CONGRESSMAN, THE OTHER ONE IS A *SENATOR.*

THEY *WORK* FOR BLOOD AND HE'S TRYING TO GET THEM *RE-ELECTED.*

BLOOD RUNS *ZANDIA* --AND ZANDIA NEEDS ARMS TO FIGHT A GROUP CALLED *THE BROTHERHOOD OF EVIL.*

THESE THREE ARE ON THE *ARMS COMMITTEE* -- AND THEY'RE SETTING UP A *TREATY* WITH ZANDIA TO SELL BLOOD THE *WEAPONS* HE NEEDS.

HOLD IT. DID YOU *HEAR* SOMETHING?

IF BLOOD *GETS* THOSE WEAPONS, THERE WILL BE *WAR.* THOUSANDS WILL DIE.

I--I CAN'T *ALLOW* THAT TO HAPPEN.

HEAR *WHAT*, ROBIN?

A SCRAPING SOUND-- HOLD IT.

LORD!

MOVE IT!

BA-WHAMMMM!

9

ROBIN, ARE YOU *OKAY*?

YEAH, YOU SEE *WHO* *DID* THIS?

HE'S RIGHT IN *FRONT* OF ME, TRYING TO *ESCAPE*.

HE WON'T GET *FAR*.

STARFIRE LUNGES FORWARD, EYES NARROWED IN ANGER, TEETH CLENCHED IN HATE.

BUT...

SKA-BLAMMM!

SHE SENSES THE *PAIN* IN ROBIN'S VOICE AND PROMISES HERSELF THAT THIS WOULD-BE KILLER WILL *PAY* FOR THIS DEED.

WHOEVER DID THIS *MINED* THE DOORWAY, PROBABLY WITH *ELECTRIC* *SENSORS*.

DON'T GO AFTER HIM *YOURSELF*, ROBIN. HE'S *DANGEROUS*.

DON'T WORRY ABOUT *ME*. I CAN HANDLE MYSELF.

NO GOOD. HE WAS *PREPARED*.

HE'S *GONE*.

MAYBE I CAN CHASE *AFTER* HIM. I'M ALL RIGHT NOW. I JUST HAD THE *WIND* KNOCKED OUT OF ME, THAT'S ALL.

DON'T BOTHER. WE KNOW *WHO* HE WAS WORKING FOR.

WELL, MISS *SNOW*, WHAT *NOW*?

LOOK, IF BLOOD *KNOWS* I'VE TURNED AGAINST HIM, HE'LL FIND SOME WAY TO *KILL* ME.

PLEASE, YOU'VE *GOT* TO *HELP* ME.

I'LL CONFESS TO *EVERYTHING*! JUST SAVE ME.

10

WHAT'S THIS *BROTHERHOOD OF EVIL*?

THE TITANS *FOUGHT* THEM *SEVERAL MONTHS* AGO. THEY'RE AN INTERNATIONAL *TERRORIST GROUP*--

--AND THEY COME COMPLETE WITH *SUPER-POWERS.*

SOUNDS LIKE THEY'RE A MILLION LAUGHS. WHAT'RE THEY *AFTER?*

BROTHER BLOOD'S *POWER.* THEY MEAN TO GET IT THROUGH ONE OF THE TITANS... *RAVEN!*

ROBIN, I THINK YOU'D BETTER--

BUT EVEN BEFORE ADRIAN CHASE CAN COMPLETE HIS THOUGHT, *ROBIN* AND *STARFIRE* ARE GONE...

THEIR FRIEND IS IN *TROUBLE.*

UPTOWN: HIS NAME IS *VICTOR STONE* AND, SEVERAL YEARS AGO, HIS BODY WAS DESTROYED IN A LABORATORY ACCIDENT. HIS LIFE, HOWEVER, WAS SAVED BY HIS FATHER WHO TURNED HIM INTO A THING THAT IS HALF MAN / HALF MACHINE --A *CYBORG.*

THOUGH HIS BODY WAS SAVED, HIS MIND SEETHED WITH ANGER TOWARD HIS FREAKISH APPEARANCE--

--UNTIL HE BECAME A MEMBER OF *THE NEW TEEN TITANS.*

--UNTIL HE MET A YOUNG WOMAN NAMED *SARAH SIMMS,* A TEACHER OF HANDICAPPED CHILDREN WHO SAW *PAST* HIS PROSTHETICALLY-ENHANCED BODY TO THE MAN *INSIDE.*

IN THE PAST MONTHS, THEY HAVE BECOME *GOOD FRIENDS.*

YES, WHO *IS* IT?

AND, VICTOR *THINKS,* PERHAPS EVEN *MORE.*

UH, MY NAME'S VIC STONE. THIS IS *SARAH'S* APARTMENT, ISN'T IT?

VICTOR? OH, I'M *SORRY*... I DIDN'T SEE THE *METAL* SIDE OF YOUR FACE.

PLEASE, COME IN. SARAH'S TOLD ME ALL *ABOUT* YOU. I'M *MARK WRIGHT.*

SPECIAL OLYMPICS

YOUR SHIRT... YOU *WORK* WITH SARAH.

USED TO. WE SET UP HER CENTER TOGETHER SEVERAL YEARS AGO.

SIT DOWN, VIC --SARAH'S OUT SHOPPING FOR THE *PARTY* TONIGHT.

11

THIS IS REALLY A *PLEASURE*. SARAH'S SO *FOND* OF YOU.

OH, I WENT DOWN TO WASHINGTON ABOUT A YEAR AGO TO OPEN ANOTHER CENTER *THERE*.

YEAH, WE MAKE A GREAT *TEAM*.

SAY, HOWCUM I HAVEN'T SEEN *YOU* AT THE CENTER? I'VE BEEN *WORKIN'* THERE SOMETIMES.

I TELL YOU, BEING *APART* FROM SARAH'S BEEN *TERRIBLE*.

Y'KNOW, WE PARTED RIGHT AFTER WE GOT *ENGAGED*. BUT HER WORK KEPT HER UP HERE.

EN-ENGAGED?

FOR A *YEAR* NOW. WE TALK ALL THE TIME BY *PHONE*.

ENGAG-- HUH?

UHH... JUST PICKED UP MY INTERNAL *ALARM*. SOMETHING'S WRONG AT *TITAN'S TOWER*.

SOMETHING *WRONG*, VICTOR?

LOOK, GIVE THIS TO *SARAH*. WISH HER *HAPPY NEW YEAR* FOR ME.

I'M SO SORRY YOU CAN'T *STAY*. SARAH WAS HOPING YOU'D BE HERE.

TELL HER I GOTTA GO *SAVE THE WORLD* OR SOMETHIN'.

IT'S BEEN *GREAT*, VIC, WE'VE GOT TO TALK *MORE* SOME DAY.

YEAH, SURE.

7313

HE LEAVES, NOT AT ALL HAPPY.

HADDA BE *CRAZY* THINKIN' WE MEANT THAT WAY TO EACH OTHER.

WHERE WAS YOUR *MIND*, STONE?

WHAT'VE YOU BEEN *THINKIN'* 'BOUT ALL THESE MONTHS?

SHE WAS A *FRIEND*, MADE ME FEEL GOOD INSIDE AN' I THOUGHT WE *LOVED* EACH OTHER MORE'N JUST FRIENDS DO.

NOT *ANGRY* AT HER. NOT EVEN *MAD* AT HER. AIN'T *HER* FAULT.

IT'S *MINE*! *MINE*!

12

WHERE IS WONDER GIRL? THE ANSWER LIES *HERE*, WITHIN THIS SKY-SCRAPING *RESTAURANT...*

THE RAINBOW

ROCKEFELLER PLAZA

MR. *LONG?* AHH, I SEE YOUR *RESERVATION.*

PLEASE FOLLOW ANDRE. HE WILL SEE YOU TO YOUR *TABLE.*

THANK YOU, ENRIQUE.

THIS IS *GORGEOUS,* TERRY. I'VE NEVER BEEN HERE BEFORE.

A CIRCULAR RESTAURANT SO YOU CAN SEE ALL ACROSS *MANHATTAN.*

TERRY, DON'T YOU THINK IT'S A TAD *EXPENSIVE?*

HONEY, THIS IS NEW YEAR'S EVE. I DIDN'T *CARE* ABOUT THE COST.

THIS, MY BEAUTIFUL LOVE, IS A VERY *SPECIAL* NIGHT FOR ME.

AND YOU WON'T TELL ME *WHY.* I CAN SEE THAT "I *KNOW SOMETHING YOU DON'T KNOW*" LOOK.

MY *DEAR,* YOU'LL FIND OUT SOON ENOUGH.

SAINT PETER'S CATHEDRAL:

THE PEWS ARE *EMPTY* NOW, THE DOOR HAS BEEN *LOCKED.*

BUT SEALED PORTALS ARE NO BARRIER TO THE DIMENSION-TRAVELING POWERS OF *RAVEN.*

RAVEN NEEDS TO BE ALONE. SHE NEEDS TO THINK, CONTEMPLATE WHO SHE IS...

AND, EVEN MORE... *WHY* SHE IS.

AND THIS CHURCH, ALTHOUGH ALIEN TO ONE WHO WAS RAISED IN THE DIMENSION-TOSSED LAND OF *AZARATH,* IS STILL A PLACE *CONDUSIVE* TO SUCH THOUGHT.

AND TO SUCH *PRAYER.*

15

70

WHY CAN I NOT *LOVE?*

WHY CAN I NOT *HATE?*

WHY CAN I NOT *FEEL?*

WHY AM I *DENIED* THE EMOTIONS ALL OTHERS POSSESS?

CAN I *HELP* YOU?

I--I AM SORRY. I AM NOT OF THIS FAITH. I DO NOT *BELONG* HERE.

OF COURSE YOU DO. IF SOMETHING IS WRONG, MAYBE I CAN *HELP.*

WILL YOU *LET* ME?

N-NO... IT IS IMPOSSIBLE. YOU CANNOT UNDERSTAND WHAT IS *WRONG* WITH ME.

FRANKLY YOU'D BE SURPRISED. PLEASE, RAVEN, GIVE ME A *CHANCE.*

YOU *KNOW* ME?

I READ THE PAPERS. I WATCH TV. IF YOU PROMISE NOT TO TELL, I EVEN ENJOY AN OCCASIONAL *VIDEO GAME.*

WE'RE NOT SEQUESTERED IN *DARK ABBEYS* ANY MORE.

PLEASE, STAY. EVERYONE IS *WELCOME* HERE.

EVEN *SATAN'S* DAUGHTER?

FATHER, SHE *CANNOT* BE HELPED.

COME TO US, RAVEN.

WHAT?!?

YOU KNOW EVENTUALLY WE'LL *GET* WHAT WE CAME FOR. WHY NOT JUST COME WITH US *PEACEFULLY?*

RAVEN FEELS THE THUNDER SCREAMING IN HER SOUL. SHE *SPEAKS* EVEN BEFORE SHE THINKS...

NEVER!

16

BECAUSE OF YOU, I ALMOST *KILLED* KID FLASH.

I WILL NEVER LET YOU *MANIPULATE* MY MIND AGAIN.

STOP!

THIS IS NOT THE PLACE TO *FIGHT!*

OH? SINCE WHEN HAVE *YOU* WORRIED ABOUT THE ARENA OF BATTLE?

DESPITE WHAT YOU *BELIEVE* ME TO BE, I WILL NOT DEFILE A *TEMPLE* OF WORSHIP.

LET US *DISCUSS* OUR DISAGREEMENT... OUTSIDE.

N-NO...I...I DO NOT FIGHT... I *CANNOT* FIGHT...

LEAVE ME ALONE! FOR AZAR'S SAKE -- *LEAVE ME ALONE!!*

SUDDENLY RAVEN IS VERY FRIGHTENED. SHE REALIZES *SHE* WAS THE ONE ANXIOUS FOR BATTLE.

AFRAID, SHE VANISHES, EVEN AS THE BROTHERHOOD OF EVIL GIVES CHASE...

...LEAVING BEHIND A VERY TROUBLED FATHER PETER MALLORY.

SHE WAS READY TO RESORT TO *VIOLENCE.*

HE SENSES SOMEHOW WHAT RAVEN *MEANT* WHEN SHE ASKED--"EVEN SATAN'S DAUGHTER?"

⑰

NEW YEAR'S EVE IN TIMES SQUARE HAS BECOME A NATIONAL TRADITION. MILLIONS AWAIT THE FALLING GLOBE, A HERALD OF HOPE FOR A BETTER TIME TO COME...

WELL, THE EXCITEMENT IS *BUILDING* DOWN THERE, JANE?

11:57:00

YOU'RE *RIGHT*, DICK. IN FACT, THE COUNTDOWN HAS ALREADY *BEGUN*. EVERYONE'S HAVING A *BALL* TONIGHT.

11:59:01

AND *SPEAKING* OF BALLS, WHEN OUR GOLDEN BALL DESCENDS, THAT SIGN WILL OFFICIALLY LIGHT UP THE NEW YEAR.

11:59:15

LET'S JOIN THE COUNTDOWN. 10, 9, 8, 7, 6, 5...

11:59:56

...I TELL YOU, EACH YEAR THE CROWD SEEMS TO *GROW*.

WHY, I CAN SEE PEOPLE PUSHED ALL THE WAY BACK TO *51ST* STREET.

3, 2...

11:59:59

THE BALL STOPPED *MOVING*... AND THE SIGN--

12:00:00

SOMETHING'S WRONG. THE SIGN'S NOT *LIGHTING*!!

I'VE HAD *LIVELIER* NEW YEAR'S EVES HANGING AROUND CEMETERIES!

WHY AIN'T WE *DOIN'* SOMETHING? RAVEN'S *LOST* OUT THERE?

YOU TELL ME WHAT TO *DO!* WHERE DO WE *GO?*

RAVEN COULD'VE TELEPORTED *ANYWHERE*.

WHY DON'T WE JUST *FORGET* HER? WE SHOULD BE LOOKING FOR THE BROTHERHOOD OF EVIL.

AND THEY WANT *RAVEN*. FORGET *THAT*, FLEET-FEET.

C'MON, ARE WE JUST GONNA WATCH *TV?* LORD, YOU PEOPLE ARE *DULL*.

WE COULD ALWAYS HEAD UP TO MY ROOM AND *NECK*.

DON'T MAKE ME *SICK*.

HEY, HOW COME THE *SIGN* DIDN'T LIGHT? IT ALWAYS LIGHTS UP?

IF THIS IS HOW IT'S *BEGINNING*, I DON'T WANT TO KNOW FROM *1983*.

18

CAN ANYONE *ELSE* SEE IT? THE SCREEN'S *SHIMMERING* NOW...

I DON'T BELIEVE IT!

1983

PINCH MY CHEEKS AND CALL ME GORGEOUS! IT'S *RAVEN!*

I *TOLD* YOU, RAVEN'S GONE *CRAZY.* MAYBE NOW YOU'LL BELIEVE ME.

MEANWHILE...

WHERE *IS* SHE?

MY COMPUTERIZED FETISH TRACED HER TO THIS AREA... IT CAN'T *PIN-POINT* HER EXACT LOCATION.

WH-WHAT *ARE* THEY?

OH, GOD! *LOOK!*

LET ME *OUTTA* HERE!

NO GOOD. MY SOUL-SELF *FRIGHTENED* THEM ...BUT THE BROTHERHOOD HAS CAUSED THEM TO *PANIC.*

THEIR FEARS... HURT... ME...

...MUST *STOP* THEM... TO GET THEM *AWAY* FROM HERE BEFORE THE PEOPLE ARE *HURT...*

...BEFORE I AM *DESTROYED* BY ALL THOSE EMOTIONS.

DERE!

SH-SHE COMES AT *ME?* WELL, SHE WILL NOT FIND ME A STANDING TARGET.

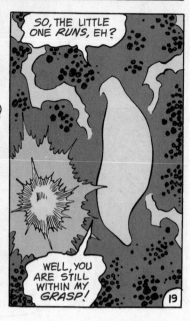

SO, THE LITTLE ONE *RUNS,* EH?

WELL, YOU ARE STILL WITHIN MY *GRASP!*

19

NO, FRÄULEIN -- I AM *NOT*.

I AM PURE *PROTOPLASM*... NOT AT ALL *HUMAN*.

YOUR SOUL CANNOT *CONFINE* ME.

RAVEN SCREAMS AS HER SOUL-SELF SEEMINGLY SHATTERS...

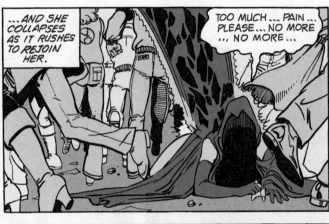

...AND SHE COLLAPSES AS IT RUSHES TO REJOIN HER.

TOO MUCH... PAIN... PLEASE... NO MORE ... NO MORE...

HI, GUYS -- YOU HEAR THE CIRCUS IS IN TOWN AND THEY NEED A NEW *FREAK SHOW?*

DEY *FOUND* US.

OF COURSE THEY DID. DIDN'T YOU *EXPECT* THEY WOULD?

HURRY AND TAKE THE *GIRL*... SHE'S THE ONLY ONE WE WANT TODAY.

NO WAY, LADY.

DER YOUNG ONE -- DER GIRL... THIS IS HER DOING.

BRAMM SLAMM

YOU CATCH ON *QUICK*, TERRA.

NOT BAD, KID.

YEAH, I KNOW. WHAT'RE YOU DOIN' TO HOLD UP *YOUR* END?

DID YOU *HEAR* THAT? THEY WANT *RAVEN.*

WELL, LET THEM *TRY!*

KOMAND'R TRIES *KIDNAPPING* ME... THESE FOOLS TRY TAKING *RAVEN.*

I'M *SICK* OF THESE SCUM!

SKREEEEE

20

FRAN? YOU SHOULDN'T HAVE GOTTEN *INVOLVED!* YOU'RE NOT *ONE* OF US.

HEY, *IGNORE* BALLOON-BOD, WAY TO *GO*, KID. MAYBE YOU'RE NOT SUCH A *WIMP* AFTER ALL.

KNOCK IT OFF, TERRA. STARFIRE'S *RIGHT*, FRAN... WE CAN'T LET YOU TAKE THE *RISK.*

THIS IS *OUR* JOB.

I'M *SORRY*, ALL OF YOU-- BUT I HAVE TO *DO* THIS.

WHERE'S *KID FLASH?* PLEASE, PHOBIA, *TELL* ME, OR I'LL HAVE THESE PIPES START *SQUEEZING* YOU UNTIL YOU DO.

I WOULD BE A FOOL TO *ANTAGONIZE* HER... AND EVEN *MORE* OF A FOOL IF I *GAVE IN* TO HER DEMANDS.

STILL, THERE IS *ANOTHER* WAY TO FREE MYSELF WITHOUT TAKING THE RISK OF CONTROLLING THE *TITANS* THEMSELVES.

TO SPREAD MY POWERS SO WIDE WILL *HURT*... HURT FAR TOO MUCH, BUT WE MUST RETURN TO *ZANDIA* WITHOUT DELAY...

HEY, THE WICKED WITCH OF THE WEST IS *UP* TO SOMETHING...

THE CROWD'S LOOKING AT US LIKE *WE'RE* THE BAD GUYS HERE. I DON'T *GET* IT.

TAKE A *LOOK*, PAL-- THAT GROUP'S BEEN *SCARED* SINCE OUR FIGHT BEGAN--

--PHOBIA *INCREASED* THEIR NATURAL FEAR...

DAMN. I DIDN'T THINK SHE COULD *DO* THAT.

THEN YOU'D BETTER *START* THINKIN'--LIKE ABOUT HOW WE'RE GONNA *SURVIVE* THIS.

SHE'S MADE 'EM SEE US LIKE WE'RE SOME KINDA *MONSTERS.*

STARFIRE! DON'T DO ANYTHING STUPID! *STARFIRE!*

DON'T *WORRY*, ROB--SHE KNOWS WHAT SHE'S *DOING.*

I JUST HOPE THE *REST* OF US DO.

22

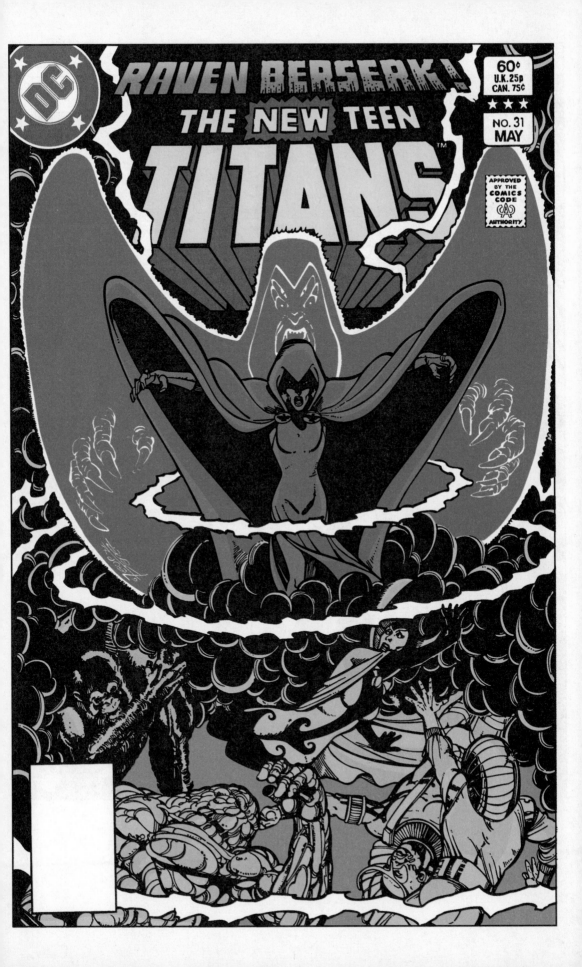

BUT *BOTH* OF YOU WERE TAKEN BY *WARP*. IS SHE *OKAY*?

STARFIRE, PLEASE. *I'LL* HANDLE THIS.

WHERE *IS* SHE?

I'M NOT *SURE*. I WAS KNOCKED OUT. LOOK, RAVEN ALMOST *KILLED* ME...

SHE'S NOT *ONE* OF US. SHE'S *NEVER* BEEN ONE OF US.

FORGET HER.

WHOA THERE, FLEET-FEET. I *SAW* WHAT HAPPENED, REMEMBER?

SHE WAS TAKEN OVER BY *PHOBIA*, AND MAN -- I KNOW WHAT *THAT* FEELS LIKE.

HE'S *RIGHT*, WAL-- UH, KID FLASH. *I* SAW IT, TOO.

FRAN, PLEASE DON'T *DO* THIS TO ME.

YOU DIDN'T FEEL THE *EVIL* IN RAVEN'S SOUL-SELF. BUT I DID. AND I'M *SCARED*.

LET ME UNDERSTAND THIS, THEY'RE ALL *FRIENDS*, HUH?

UHHH... NO COMPRENDO INGLES.

LOGAN!!

WELLLL, THEY'RE *SUPPOSED* TO BE.

I *THINK*.

LISTEN, SPEEDY, YOU'RE NOT A *REGULAR* TITAN, SO WHY DON'T YOU TAKE YOUR BLASTED ARROWS AND *STICK* 'EM?

DON'T SAY THAT. IT'S NOT *NICE*.

AHHH, JUST LIKE THE *OLD* DAYS.

NOW I REMEMBER WHY I *LEFT*.

LISSEN, I DON'T CARE IF YOU TWO TEAR EACH OTHER INTO LITTLE *PIECES*--

--BUT DO IT BACK AT THE TOWER -- IN *PRIVATE*.

THEY LEAVE...

...BUT NOT ONE OF THEM IS HAPPY.

2

FIVE TITANS, ONE RESERVIST AND ONE FRIEND... EXHAUSTED FROM THEIR BATTLE WITH THE *BROTHERHOOD OF EVIL*, THEY DRAG THEMSELVES BACK TO THEIR EAST RIVER ISLAND HEADQUARTERS...

STARFIRE IS THE *FIRST* TO ENTER, AND THE FIRST TO SPY A FAMILIAR RED-AND-BLUE UNIFORM...

HI, WHERE HAVE YOU *BEEN*?

WHERE HAVE *WE* BEEN? WE TRIED *CALLING* YOU.

ARE YOU *OKAY*? WHAT WAS *WRONG*?

I WAS WORRIED SOMETHING *HAPPENED*.

WELL, STARFIRE, IN A WAY I GUESS SOMETHING *DID* HAPPEN.

TERRY LONG *PROPOSED.*

HE WANTS TO *MARRY* ME.

WONDER GIRL, DIDN'T YOU HEAR THE *EMERGENCY SIGNAL*?

MARRY *YOU*?

X'HAL! THAT'S *WONDERFUL!* IT'S INCREDIBLE!

WHEN WILL IT *HAPPEN*? HOW DID HE PROPOSE? PLEASE-- DON'T LEAVE OUT *ANYTHING*.

HECK, SHE COULD HAVE BEEN *MINE*. SHE'S BEEN DYING FOR MY BONES EVER SINCE WE *MET*.

LOGAN, DON'T YOU *EVER* STOP WITH THE JOKES?

OH, NUTS-- JUST WHAT I NEED. NOW *VIC'S* FLIPPED OUT.

4

83

THAT'S REALLY GREAT. I'M SO GLAD FOR YOU.

YOU DIDN'T *TELL* US-- WHEN'S THE HAPPY *DAY?*

HOLD IT... I HAVEN'T GIVEN HIM MY *ANSWER* YET.

SOMETHING *WRONG?*

OH, NO-- THERE'S ABSOLUTELY *NO ONE* I'D RATHER SPEND MY LIFE WITH THAN *TERRY*--

--WE *LOVE* EACH OTHER. WE *CARE* FOR EACH OTHER. THAT'S NOT THE *PROBLEM.*

IT'S *ME*, ROBIN --I--I ALWAYS HOPED I'D FIND OUT WHO I *REALLY* WAS BEFORE I GOT MARRIED...

I--I DON'T KNOW WHAT TO *DO.*

HEY, IT'LL WORK OUT. MAYBE I CAN *HELP*, OKAY?

WELL, MY ONE-TIME HEART-THROB, IF YOU HAVEN'T GIVEN HIM AN *ANSWER*, REMEMBER--*I'M* AVAILABLE.

THANKS, PAL --I'LL CONSIDER YOUR *OFFER.*

YEAH, LET'S ALL SAY *CONGRATULATIONS* AND GET DOWN TO THE MATTER AT HAND.

I'M SORRY... I THINK WE ALL *FORGOT.*

I KNOW. RAVEN AND I WERE TELEPORTED TO ZANDIA-- THAT'S THE LAST I *SAW* OF HER.

IF YOU REALLY DO WANT TO *FIND* HER -- I'D SUGGEST WE START *THERE.*

MINUTES LATER THE TITANS' T-JET STREAKS ACROSS THE NEW YORK SKIES, HEADING ON A COURSE, DUE EAST...

THE SILENCE ON BOARD IS THICK AND ALMOST DEAFENING.

THERE ARE PROBLEMS THAT MUST BE WORKED OUT, PROBLEMS THAT, IF LEFT TO FESTER, COULD RIP THE TITANS ASUNDER.

MEANWHILE, ON THE BALTIC ISLAND OF ZANDIA...

5

...IN THE HEADQUARTERS OF -- THE BROTHERHOOD OF EVIL...

MONSIEUR BRAIN, HAS ZE NEW BROTHERHOOD WORKED OUT AS YOU HAD *HOPED?*

AH, MONSIEUR MALLAH, THEY ARE NOT THE *ORIGINAL* BROTHERHOOD, BUT THEY WILL *DO*...

THEY ARE STILL YOUNG. THEY STILL THINK MORE WITH THEIR *HEARTS* THAN WITH THEIR BRAINS.

BUT THEY WILL EITHER LEARN OR THEY WILL *DIE.* ONE WAY OR ANOTHER, THINGS WILL WORK OUT.

BUT WILL ZEY INTERFERE WITH YOUR *PLANS?* YOU HAVE WORKED SO *HARD*...

DO NOT PUT THEM DOWN, MONSIEUR MALLAH. THEY ARE NEW, BUT THEY ARE *GOOD.*

THEY WILL GET ME WHAT I *WANT*--

--THE SECRET OF BROTHER BLOOD!

SHE AWAKENS. NOW WE CAN *PROCEED.*

LET *ME* TRY FIRST. I ALREADY KNOW HER WORST *FEAR*... I CAN USE IT TO *LOOSEN* HER TONGUE.

NO, PHOBIA-- *I* WILL BE DER FIRST, DER BRAIN WANTED ME TO *WORK* WIF DIS TITAN.

AH, ZIS SHALL BE *INTERESTING,* NON? THIS ONE, SHE HAS ZE 'BEAUTE DU DIABLE' -- THE BEAUTY OF THE *DEVIL;* THE BLOOM AND FRESHNESS OF YOUTH.

SHE WEEL NOT BE AN *EASY* ONE TO CRACK, NON.

6

YOU KNOW THE SECRET OF BROTHER BLOOD. TELL US, FRÄULEIN... VE ARE NOT IN DER MOOD FOR *GAMES.*

YOU ARE MAKING A *MISTAKE,* PLASMUS--

I WILL NOT PERMIT YOU TO *HURT* ME.

STOP!

THERE!--AS FOR THE *REST* OF YOU, I KNOW NOTHING OF BROTHER BLOOD.., YOUR FIGHT IS NOT WITH ME OR THE TITANS.

YOU WOULD DO WELL TO LEAVE US *ALONE.*

I AM *SORRY,* LITTLE GIRL, BUT THAT CANNOT *BE.*

MY *STOMACH!* IT IS *BURNING UP!*

MY DEAR RAVEN, I CAN *CURE* YOUR ILLS IF YOU WILL LET ME...

...OR I CAN *INCREASE* THEM IF YOU ARE *STUBBORN.*

MY COMPUTER FETISH CAN BE YOUR *FRIEND*-- OR YOUR *KILLER.* WHICH SHALL IT BE?

TALK! TELL US THE SECRET OF BLOOD'S *POWER!*

I...CANNOT THINK ...THE PAIN CUTS THROUGH ME LIKE A *BLADE.*

AZAR-- WHY? WHY ARE MY HANDS, WHICH CAN SOOTHE THE PAINS OF OTHERS, SO POWERLESS TO CURE *ME?*

WHY, AZAR? WHY?

7

MONSIEUR BRAIN, IT IS AS I FEARED. ZE NEW ONES USE THEIR POWERS SO *CRUDELY.*

WAIT, MONSIEUR MALLAH-- GIVE THEM A *CHANCE.* SHOULD THEY FAIL, *THEN* I WILL INTERFERE.

ALLOW THEM TO LEARN HOW BEST TO *WIELD* THEIR STRENGTHS.

IT'S NO GOOD... IF I *CONTINUE* USING THE FETISH, I WOULD *KILL* HER. WE'D LEARN *NOTHING* THAT WAY.

IT IS UP TO *YOU,* PHOBIA. DO NOT *FAIL* THE BRAIN.

IF I HAD BEEN THE FIRST, THE INFORMATION WOULD *ALREADY* BE OURS.

MY DEAR RAVEN-- ONE LAST CHANCE-- *TALK!*

I--I KNOW *NOTHING!*

VERY WELL, IF YOU INSIST ON REMAINING SO STUBBORN, I WILL DO WHAT *MUST* BE DONE.

YOU ARE A SAD CASE, GIRL-- YOUR FEARS ARE SO *RIFE.*

THE PROBLEM WITH YOU IS NOT FINDING YOUR WEAKNESS, BUT *CHOOSING* WHICH WEAKNESS TO EXPLOIT.

YOUR FATHER *TRIGON?* NO-- I HAVE ALREADY PLAYED OUT THAT HAND.

I CAN EXPLOIT EACH FEAR ONLY *ONCE.*

PERHAPS YOUR LUDICROUS *SHYNESS...* SHALL WE PLUNGE YOU INTO THE CENTER OF A MILLION SOULS?

WAIT... WAIT, I HAVE IT. SO DELICIOUS.

YOU ARE AN *EMPATH*-- YOU THRIVE ON THE EMOTIONS OF OTHERS.

NO, PHOBIA-- *DON'T!* FOR AZAR'S SAKE, YOU DO NOT KNOW WHAT YOU COULD *UNLEASH!*

PLEASE... IF THERE IS ANY *MERCY* IN YOUR HEART -- SHOW IT *NOW!*

DO NOT *DO* THIS TO ME!

8

...THEY ALL PLEAD WITH HER, GRAB AT HER... PULL AT HER... SCREAM AT HER!

A MILLION SOULS AND MORE RIPPING AWAY EACH PROTECTIVE BARRIER TO HER FRAGILE SOUL...

THEY ALL WANT PART OF HER ...THEY ALL WANT THAT *SAME* PART-- THE PART WHICH CAN SAVE THEM --

FOR GOD'S SAKE, RAVEN --HELP US ALL!

BUT, RAVEN KNOWS, TO SAVE THEM WOULD BE TO *DESTROY* HERSELF!

AND AGAIN RAVEN SCREAMS.

CURE ME!

SAVE ME!

SAVE ME!

THEY PICK AT HER FLESH, RIP AT HER DRESS... EXPOSE HER TO HORRORS AND SHAMES AND FEARS AND ILLNESSES AND DISEASES AND--

RAVEN SCREAMS!

EVEN AS SHE PLUNGES DEEPER INTO HER NIGHT-MARE-- EVEN AS HER GREATEST FEARS BECOME MANIFEST AND, IF POSSIBLE, GROW WORSE.

⑨

SHE IS NAKED TO THE WORLD...

BUT, AMIDST THE FLAME AND HEAT AND HELL, SHE FEELS... SERENE.

ALMOST WITHOUT UNDERSTANDING *WHY*, SHE SITS UP, CASUALLY GLANCING ABOUT HER.

AND, FOR PERHAPS THE FIRST TIME IN HER LIFE, SHE SMILES.

SHE IS ALONE, AND HER PRIVATE, PERSONAL SOUL HAS NOT BEEN VIOLATED.

THEN...

THEN, IT STARTS ALL OVER AGAIN.

AND AGAIN! AND AGAIN! *AND AGAIN!*

SHE CAN NEVER BE LEFT ALONE. SHE CAN NEVER ENJOY EVEN A MOMENT OF *PEACE*...

HER PRIVATE HORRORS EXPOSED TO ALL WHO SEE HER.

CALM?

EMOTIONS SURROUND HER, ALWAYS ATTACKING HER, ALWAYS FEEDING UPON HER, ALWAYS *DESTROYING* HER.'

AND AGAIN SHE SCREAMS. AND AGAIN SHE FALLS...

...CRASHING INTO THE DEPTHS OF HER TORTURED SOUL.

SHE KNOWS -- SHE CRIES -- SHE PLEADS -- THE GREATEST HORRORS HAVE ONLY YET BEGUN!

10

FOR A LONG TIME SHE REFUSES TO OPEN HER EYES, ALTHOUGH SHE CANNOT HELP BUT SENSE WHAT AWAITS HER IN THE DARKNESS.

SHE SEES HIM, THAT DAMNED PART OF HER SHE HAS ALWAYS SOUGHT TO DENY... THAT DAMNED PART OF HER SHE HAS ALWAYS TRIED TO REFUSE

TRIGON!

HER FATHER -- THE DAMNED THING WHO HAS KILLED HER ONLY FRIENDS.

THIS TIME... THIS ONE TIME, RAVEN DOES NOT SCREAM.

THIS TIME SHE ALLOWS HERSELF TO HATE.

THIS TIME SHE REVELS IN THE EMOTIONS WHICH SHE HAS ALWAYS HAD TO DENY.

HER FATHER -- EVIL INCARNATE -- BORN IN ANOTHER DIMEN-SION... HER FATHER WHO LIVES IN THE EBONY FOLDS OF HER LIFE-GIVING SOUL-SELF.

HER FATHER, HAND-IN-HAND WITH THE BROTHERHOOD.

...RAVEN..., WHY DID YOU LET THEM DO THIS TO ME, RAVEN...? WHY DID YOU HELP THEM KILL US?

WE LOVE YOU... I-I LOVED YOU... IS THIS HOW YOU PAY US BACK -- BY KILLING US?

IS IT, RAVEN? IS IT?

11

T-TAKE MY HAND.

MY LIFE WILL BE PASSED ON TO YOU.

YOU WILL LIVE.

YES... YES! TAKE MY HAND!

AND YOU'LL DIE, RAVEN? IS THAT IT? WILL YOU DIE?

NO!

YOU'RE DEATH.

YOU'RE EVIL!

YOU'RE EVERYTHING THAT IS WRONG!!

I'D RATHER DIE BEFORE LETTING YOU CURE ME!

BAH! SHE IS UNCONSCIOUS. WHAT DID YOU DO TO HER?

I...DO NOT KNOW, PLASMUS. I BEGAN HER NIGHTMARE. WHERE SHE LET IT TRAVEL I DO NOT KNOW.

A SHAME. I WAS POSITIVE SHE WOULD BREAK.

HMMM. PERHAPS SHE WAS TELLING THE TRUTH. PERHAPS SHE DOESN'T KNOW ANYTHING.

IS THAT POSSIBLE?

NO, PLASMUS -- SHE KNOWS, ALTHOUGH SHE IS UNAWARE OF THAT FACT.

VERY WELL....LOCK HER AWAY. ATTACH HER TO A MIND-DAMPENER TO PREVENT HER FROM TELEPORTING TO FREEDOM.

IF I'M TO LEARN THE SECRET OF BROTHER BLOOD'S POWERS, I MUST-- THINK.

12

THERE IS SILENCE AS THE T-JET SPEEDS ACROSS A FROTHY ATLANTIC...

THE SILENCE OF CONCERN FOR A TEAMMATE...

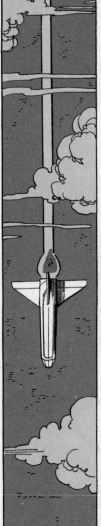

... AND THE SILENCE OF PERSONAL CONCERNS AS WELL.

THEN...

WHAT'S *WRONG,* CAN-HEAD? SOMEONE STICK YOUR DOG IN A GARBAGE DISPOSAL?

TO USE *YOUR* WORDS, TERRA -- MIND YOUR OWN *BUSINESS.*

SOMETHING *IS* WRONG, ISN'T THERE, VIC?

GIVE YOUR GIRLFRIEND SOME HICKEYS AND LEAVE ME *ALONE.*

HEY, VIC-- C'MON. LEVEL.

YEAH, OKAY, LOGAN. IT'S SARAH ... I MET HER-- *FIANCE.*

OH.

MAN, I'VE BEEN A *FOOL* THINKING WE HAD SOMETHING *SPECIAL.*

HOW COULD SHE EVER CARE FOR A WALKING *JUNK PILE?*

ROBIN?

NOT *NOW,* STARFIRE.

YES--*NOW,* ROBIN, I INTEND TO TALK TO YOU. I'D LIKE TO *HELP* YOU. I WANT TO.

STARFIRE-- PLEASE...

LISTEN TO ME, ROBIN--YOU TREAT ME LIKE I'M *STUPID.*

BUT I'M *NOT*--I'M AS WELL-EDUCATED AS *ANYONE* HERE--IT'S JUST YOUR EARTH *CUSTOMS* THAT I CAN NEVER FATHOM--

IF YOU *LOVE* SOMEONE ON TAMARAN, YOU LIVE FOR THEM AND THEY FOR YOU.

YOU'RE *RIGHT,* STARFIRE--I *DO* TREAT YOU LIKE-- WELL, ALL WRONG. I'M SORRY.

BUT UNDERSTAND *OUR* CUSTOMS--SOMETIMES WHEN THINGS ARE GOING WRONG WE *PREFER* TO BE LEFT ALONE.

DO YOU UNDER-STAND?

NO, BUT I WILL DO WHAT YOU *WANT.*

13

MEANWHILE... COME, PHOBIA-- LOOK HOW ZE BRAIN AND MONSIEUR MALLAH HANDLE THE GIRL.

PLEASE, MADEMOISELLE, YOU MUST *AID* US IN STOPPING ZIS BROTHER BLOOD.

YOU DO NOT KNOW HOW *EVIL* HE IS.

HE EES TAMPERING WITH THE *ELECTIONS* OF YOUR COUNTRY -- TRYING TO GAIN *WEAPONS* WITH WHICH HE CAN DECLARE *WAR.*

YOU DO NOT WANT HIM TO *SUCCEED,* NO?

N-NO...

MADEMOISELLE-- THIS BROTHER BLOOD WILL CAUSE MANY *DEATHS* --

-- BUT THEY CAN *ALL* BE AVOIDED IF YOU HELP US FIND THE *SOURCE* OF HIS POWER.

THE BRAIN'S WORDS ARE UNNATURALLY CALMING--ALMOST REASSURING. RAVEN HAS *NO* IDEA WHY SHE *BELIEVES* HIM.

ONE IS AN *ANIMAL*--HIGHLY EVOLVED BUT STILL A *BEAST*...

THE OTHER IS A HUMAN BRAIN IN A *METAL* CASING.

I--I CANNOT 'READ' THESE TWO AND LEARN IF THEY SPEAK THE TRUTH, YET I *WANT* TO BELIEVE...

FASCINATING...LOOK AT THE GIRL, SHE IS *CONSIDERING* THEIR WORDS.

SHE *BELIEVES* THEM.

MAYBE ZE BRAIN *HAS* SOMETHING TO TEACH US AFTER ALL.

BUT I *KNOW* NOTHING.

NO, MADEM-OISELLE, YOU *KNOW* THE TRUTH...

...BUT IT IS *BURIED* IN YOU. COME, I SHALL *EXPLAIN.*

14

WHEN YOU BATTLED BROTHER BLOOD, YOUR SOUL-SELF *ENVELOPED* HIM, AND YET HE STEPPED RIGHT *THROUGH* IT.

AT THAT MOMENT, UNKNOWN TO YOU, YOU ABSORBED *KNOWLEDGE.*

HOW DO YOU *KNOW* THIS?

I KNOW... PLEASE *TRUST* ME.

AND, RAVEN DOES... IT *MUST* BE TRUE... I AM REMEMBERING CAVERNS... DEEP *PITS*... THERE IS DARKNESS BROKEN WITH HIGH FLAMES... FLAMES THAT HOLD THE STENCH OF BRIMSTONE.

YES... YES... THAT IS IT. *LEAD* ME TO THAT PIT...

THEN BLOOD'S SECRET SHALL BE *MINE* AS WELL!

WHY DOES SHE *STOP?*

QUIET, PHOBIA... IS THERE SOMETHING *WRONG,* RAVEN ?

NO... THE PIT IS *IN* THERE -- *I* CAN GO THERE BUT I CANNOT TAKE YOU *WITH* ME.

BAH! LEAVE DAT TO *ME!*

MY BODY IS PURE *PROTOPLASM,* IT RESPONDS TO MY EVERY COMMAND.

I CAN *BURN* A PATHWAY THROUGH THIS MOUNTAIN...

...MELTING THROUGH DIS ROCK AS IF IT WERE -- *AIR!*

I COULD *TELEPORT* AHEAD.

DERE IS A *CAVERN* AHEAD OF US.

STAY WITH US. WE SHALL BE AT MY GOAL SOON ENOUGH.

15

SO WHAT *NOW*? DO WE TAKE IN THE *SIGHTS*?

TERRA, WE CHECK OUT BROTHER BLOOD'S *CHURCH*. THEY SHOULD KNOW WHERE THE BROTHERHOOD IS *HIDING*.

OH.

ROBIN, OF THE *TEEN TITANS*?

YES, WHAT'S *WRONG*?

BY ORDER OF ZANDIA'S PRESIDENT, PERMISSION TO LAND IN ZANDIA HAS BEEN *DENIED*.

BUT WE HAVE *PROPER CLEARANCE*.

IT HAS BEEN *REVOKED*. AS YOU KNOW, OUR 'CITIZENS' ARE ALL FORMER *CRIMINALS*.

YOUR PRESENCE HERE *WORRIES* THEM.

WE DO NOT WANT TROUBLE. YOU WILL LEAVE-- *NOW*.

NO!

OUR WEAPONS --THEY *FLOAT AWAY?!?*

WE'RE NOT GOING WITH-OUT OUR *FRIEND*.

BE *CAREFUL*, FRAN.

WAY TO *GO*, SKINNY.

GENTLEMEN...

...*MY* POWERS ARE NOT SO BENIGN. DO NOT FORCE ME TO *USE* THEM.

LET US *THROUGH!*

16

IN ONE OF THE DEEPER CAVERNS BENEATH BROTHER BLOOD'S CHURCH...

MOTHER MAYHEM, OUR INNER PERIMETERS HAVE BEEN *BREACHED.*

ACCESS TO THE *REGENERATION CHAMBER* IS IMMINENT.

AND THE *MAJORITY* OF OUR FORCES ARE IN AMERICA WITH OUR *MASTER.*

BUT I SEE OUR *BACK-UP* FORCE HAS ARRIVED

GET ME CAPTAIN *HERNANDEZ* AT THE AIRPORT.

MOTHER MAYHEM, WILL THE TITANS *DO* WHAT WE WANT?

THEY *WILL.*

CAPTAIN HERNANDEZ -- A TELEPHONE MESSAGE -- FROM *BROTHER BLOOD.*

BLOOD?

CAPTAIN, ALLOW OUR GUESTS TO PASS THROUGH. WE *WANT* THEM HERE.

DO NOT WORRY, *WE* WILL DEAL WITH OUR FAIR PRESIDENT.

BUT, IS IT ALREADY *TOO LATE?*

THERE... I SENSE *THIS* IS WHAT YOU HAVE BEEN SEARCHING FOR.

BUT I *WARN* YOU -- I SENSE *EVIL.* ENTER THE PIT AND YOUR VERY *SOUL* WILL BE TORN ASUNDER.

17

SOUL? IF SUCH A THING EVER EXISTED, I LONG AGO *LOST* MINE.

MADEMOISELLE, YOUR WORDS DO NOT FRIGHTEN US. *GO.*

TREAD *CAREFULLY,* MY FRIENDS -- THE *EXISTENCE* OF THE SOUL IS NOT SOMETHING TO TAKE *LIGHTLY.*

I DO NOT FEAR ITS *LOSS,* BUT IT--

WHAT? THE GROUND SHAKES?!?

AFTER EVERYTHING I'VE DONE -- THEY'VE *COME?!!*

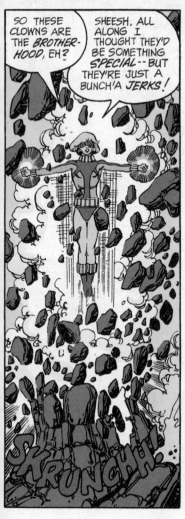

SO THESE CLOWNS ARE THE *BROTHERHOOD,* EH?

SHEESH. ALL ALONG I THOUGHT THEY'D BE SOMETHING *SPECIAL* -- BUT THEY'RE JUST A BUNCH'A *JERKS!*

SKRUNCH!!

I SEE *RAVEN...* THANK X'HAL THEY HAVEN'T *HURT* HER.

WATCH YOURSELF -- THEY'RE NOT GOING TO GIVE HER UP WITHOUT A *STRUGGLE.*

GOOD. I'M *NOT* VERY HAPPY, AND I WANT THEM TO *KNOW* THAT.

THIS IS *IT?* WE'RE ACTUALLY *HERE?*

FRAN, IF YOU'RE FRIGHTENED, YOU CAN *WAIT* FOR US.

NO. I HAVE TO *DO* THIS.

SPLASH!

THEN *WATCH* YERSELF. WE HAVEN'T GOT THE TIME TO FIGHT THEM WHILE *NURSEMAIDIN'* YOU.

18

THE BATTLE EBBS AND FLOWS LIKE AN OCEAN TIDE, FOR STARFIRE THERE COMES A PAINFUL **DEFEAT**...

...AS SHE HELPLESSLY CRUMBLES BEFORE THE COMPUTERIZED VOODOO OF HOUNGAN.

MEANWHILE, ALL RAVEN CAN DO IS WATCH IN HORROR AND PRAY TO AZAR...

RELIEVED, SHE WATCHES AS **VICTORY** IS SNATCHED FROM DEFEAT...

...AND, FOR THE MOMENT, RAVEN IS PLEASED...

STILL, SHE ALMOST SMILES AS ROBIN EASILY **DISPATCHES** HOUNGAN...

YET...SHE KNOWS BETTER THAN TO ASSUME **SUCCESS** IS AT HAND.

...AND CHANGELING DEFEATS MALLAH.

SHE SENSES AND LIVES HER TEAM-MATES' JOYS...

BUT, SOMETHING **BOTHERS** HER...

SHE IS BEGINNING TO **BASK** IN THEIR PHYSICAL VICTORIES.

SHE IS **ENTHRALLED** BY THE VIOLENCE.

SHE ANXIOUSLY **ANTICIPATES** THE CONFRONTATIONS.

AND SHE IS **FRIGHTENED**. ALL HER LIFE SHE HAS BEEN TRAINED IN PASSIVITY...IN NON-VIOLENCE...

WHY DOES SHE NOW **REVEL** IN EVERYTHING SHE DOES NOT BELIEVE?

THEN, ONCE AGAIN, SHE FEELS THE EBBING TIDE...

THE BATTLE IS ABOUT TO **CHANGE**.

⑳

AND ONE...

...BY ONE...

...BY ONE...

...THE TITANS FALL...

...DEFEATED.

AND STILL ALL RAVEN CAN DO IS WATCH IN HORROR.

HER TEAM-MATES SEEM DEAD. SHE FEELS THE HEAT SURROUNDING HER.

SHE IS MIRED IN PURGATORY...

...A HELL SHE HAS WALKED BEFORE...

HER NIGHTMARE! HER PREMONITION!

IT HAS TRAGICALLY ALL COME TRUE!

AND RAVEN SCREAMS!

21

WHILE ALL HELL BREAKS LOOSE!

YOU HAVE GONE TOO FAR,

YOU WILL HAVE TO PAY!

MON DIEU! WHAT HAS *HAPPENED* TO HER?

I-I CANNOT BELIEVE IT! *LOOK!*

SHE HAS BECOME HIM... THAT DAMNED PART OF HER SHE HAS ALWAYS SOUGHT TO *DENY*... THAT DAMNED PART OF HER SHE HAS ALWAYS TRIED TO *REFUSE.*

TRIGON!

HER FATHER--EVIL INCARNATE--BORN IN ANOTHER DIMENSION... HER FATHER WHO LIVES IN THE EBONY FOLDS OF HER LIFE-GIVING SOUL-SELF.

HER FATHER, HAND IN HAND WITH THE BROTHERHOOD.

HER FATHER--THE DAMNED THING WHO HAS *KILLED* HER ONLY FRIENDS.

22

THIS TIME... THIS ONE TIME, RAVEN DOES NOT SCREAM.

THIS TIME SHE ALLOWS HERSELF TO **HATE**.

THIS TIME SHE REVELS IN THE **EMOTIONS** WHICH SHE HAS ALWAYS HAD TO DENY.

GREAT HERA-- **NO!** RAVEN-- DON'T!

YOU DON'T KNOW WHAT YOU'RE **DOING!**

NO GOOD. SHE'S NOT **LISTENING...**

THANK HERA I GOT BACK IN TIME-- BUT IS THERE ANY WAY I CAN--

NO! SHE DOESN'T **RECOGNIZE** ME. SHE'S NO LONGER HERSELF.

EVEN THE WAY SHE'S STANDING--SO CONFIDENT... SO MUCH IN **CONTROL** OF HER POWER.

THAT'S NOT **RAVEN**--BUT IT REMINDS ME OF--

GREAT HERA!!!

NO!

23

IF TRIGON'S *CONTROLLING* HER, WE COULD ALL BE IN DANGER.

I'VE GOT TO *STOP* HIM -- GOT TO FORCE HIM *OUT OF* HER.

LISTEN TO ME, RAVEN -- FOR GOD'S SAKE -- *LISTEN!*

GET AWAY FROM ME, HUMAN! AWAY BEFORE I DESTROY YOU!

TRIGON WOULD *KILL* ME IF HE COULD -- NOT JUST THREATEN ME. IT'S NOT *TOO LATE.*

NO -- I WANT RAVEN... *RAVEN!* PLEASE... HEAR ME... DEEP IN YOUR SOUL -- HEAR ME, *LISTEN* TO ME!

YOU ARE *NOT* YOUR FATHER -- YOU ARE NOT TRIGON. YOU CAN *FIGHT* HIM!

RESIST HIM!

IF YOU *DON'T* -- YOU'LL *MURDER ALL YOUR FRIENDS!*

NO!

I WILL NOT KILL! I WILL NOT KILL! I WILL NOT KILL!

AND...

WH-WHAT *HAPPENED?*

IS RAVEN *ALL RIGHT?*

SHE TRIED TO *KILL* US... DIDN'T SHE?

N...NO...GOD PITY HER AND HELP HER --

-- SHE TRIED TO KILL *HERSELF!*

BUT YOU'RE WITH YOUR *FRIENDS* NOW, RAVEN... EVERY-THING WILL BE ALL RIGHT...

EVERYTHING WILL BE *ALL RIGHT!*

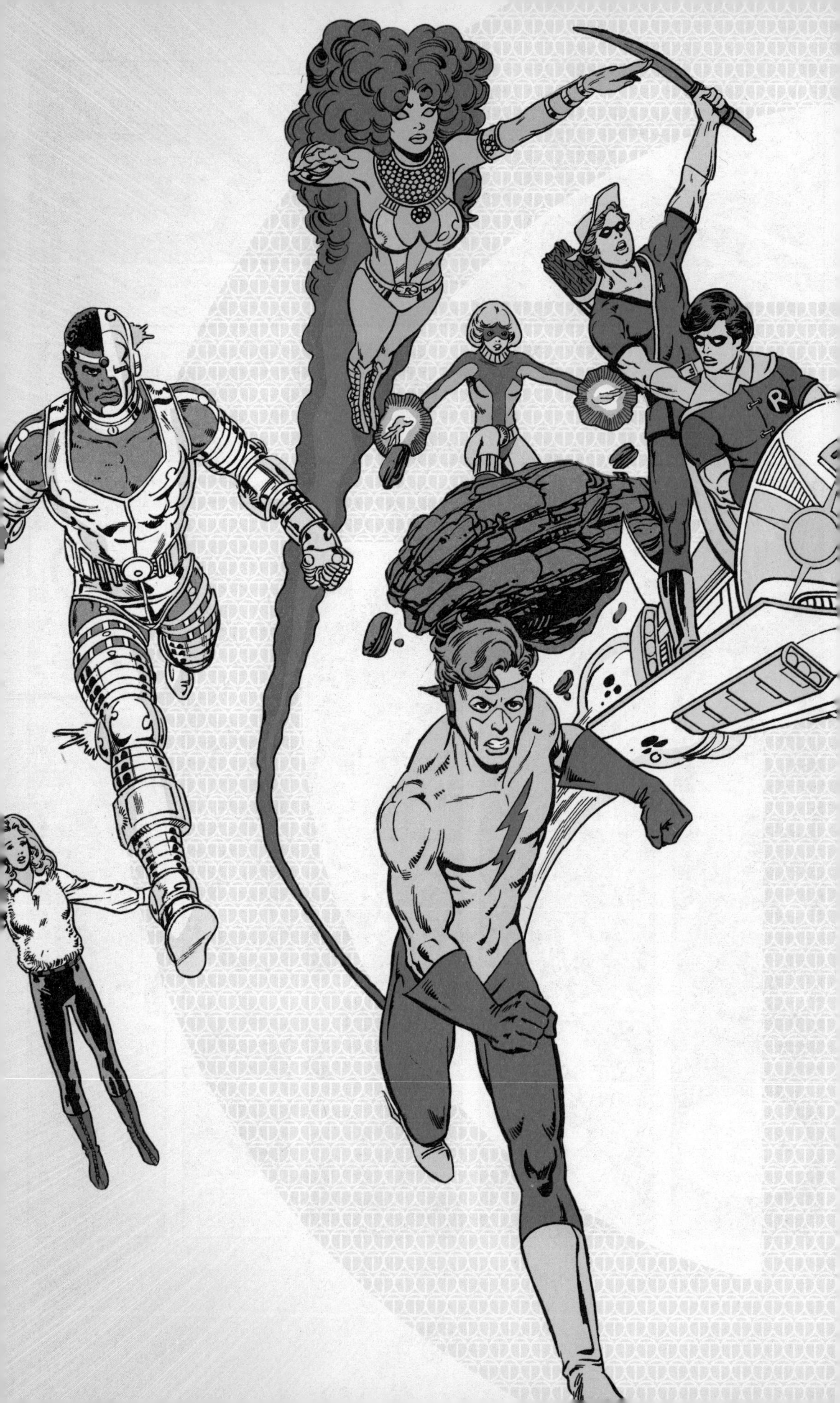

WHERE? TELL US WHERE HE HAS GONE?

YOU MUST CONTROL YOURSELF.

I CANNOT... IT IS TOO LATE.

HURRY, GAN -- LET'S GET AWAY FROM HERE

NO. NOT UNTIL I GET ANSWERS. WE'VE SEARCHED TOO LONG ALREADY.

PLEASE-- TELL US WHERE HE IS. I DON'T KNOW IF I CAN HOLD BACK MY BROTHER MUCH LONGER.

GET OUTTA HERE. WE ALREADY TOLD YA HE'S NOT HERE.

HE MOVED WEEKS AGO.

LOOK, WE TOLD A YA -- NOBODY KNOWS. HE DIDN'T SAY NOTHIN'!

LEAVE US ALONE!

I-I CANNOT!

At first it sounds like the roar of distant drums. Then the rumbling draws CLOSER...

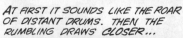

RRRRRRRRRRRRRRRRRRRRRRRRR

CLOSER...

DO YOU SEE IT? YOU HAVE NO CHOICE NOW-- RUN! LEAVE YOUR BUILDING--RUN!

STORM CLOUDS? BUT IT'S SUPPOSED TO BE SUNNY.

THEY DID IT-- THOSE KIDS!

2

DIDN'T YOU FOOLS HEAR ME? RUN! RUN!

ONCE THE CHAIN REACTION BEGINS -- OUR POWERS CAN'T BE STOPPED!!

WE'RE AS MUCH VICTIMS AS YOU ARE! RUN!

SKRAK!

I'M GETTIN' OUTTA HERE!

WH- WHAT ARE THEY DOING?

THE CRASH OF THUNDER DEAFENS THE FRIGHTENED MISSOURIANS, AS LIGHTNING CUTS A JAGGED SWATH ACROSS THE CLOUD-BLACKENED SKIES...

KKRAK!

IN AN INSTANT, THE APARTMENT HOUSE IS GONE, CRUMBLED TO SO MUCH WORTHLESS RUBBLE...

THEY RUN THEN, HIDING IN THE DARKNESS, AS FRIGHTENED AS ANY OTHER BY THE TERRIBLE DISPLAY OF THEIR AWESOME POWER...

IT HURTS, GAN?

NO, THAT'S THE THING OF IT... IT FEELS GOOD NOW.

CHAN TI WAS RIGHT. I ALMOST WANT TO USE MY POWERS... I WANT TO FEEL THE CALM THEY GIVE ME.

IT FRIGHTENS ME, TAVIS -- I THINK I HAVE TO USE MY POWERS NOW.

I KNOW WHAT YOU MEAN... I AM FEELING THOSE SENSATIONS AS WELL.

DEEP INSIDE I WANT TO HURT. I WANT TO DESTROY.

WE MUST FIND HIM BEFORE WE DO.

WHERE IS HE, BROTHER--?

WHERE IS HE?

3

THEIR MISSION IN ZANDIA IS OVER AND THE TITANS ARE *TIRED.* FOR MOST, THIS IS A TIME TO *REST...*

HE WON'T EVEN TELL ME WHAT'S *WRONG,* DICK-- DON'T YOU UNDERSTAND?-- I'D *LIKE* TO HELP. WE *ALL* WOULD.

GOD, IT'S GETTING TO BE *TOO MUCH.* I CAN'T *HACK* IT ANY LONGER.

MAYBE I NEED A *BREAK...* SOME TIME OFF TO *THINK.*

HE HELPED CONVINCE *RAVEN* TO TELL US WHAT WAS WRONG WITH HER. WHY WON'T HE TAKE HIS OWN *ADVICE?*

I'VE LIVED SO MANY *LIVES.* THE FLYING GRAYSONS. BATMAN. THE TITANS. COLLEGE. MY *OWN* ADVENTURES. NOW-- CONSIDERING WHAT'S *HAPPENED...*

MAYBE I SHOULD *QUIT* THE TITANS--! BLAST! I WISH I KNEW WHAT TO *DO.*

I'M SO HAPPY YOU'RE *BACK* WITH US, RAVEN. BUT WHY DID YOU *LEAVE* IN THE FIRST PLACE?

YOU HAVE *SEEN* ME, KORIAND'R-- I CANNOT *CONTROL* WHAT I AM.

I *COULD KILL*-- I ALMOST *DID.* I-- SHOULD *NOT* BE A *MEMBER* OF THIS GROUP.

FLASH...

I'LL *SECOND* THAT MOTION.

YEAH? WHAT *IS* IT, FRAN?

HAVE YOU *DECIDED* YET? DO YOU WANT TO COME BACK WITH ME TO *BLUE VALLEY?*

I DON'T *KNOW.*

I NEED *HELP.* I LOVE BEING WITH THE TITANS -- I REALLY *DO* --

--BUT SO MUCH OF ME DOESN'T *BELONG* HERE. I STILL THINK I NEED TIME TO BE IN *SCHOOL.* I NEED TIME TO *GROW UP.*

TRYING TO JUGGLE *TWO BALLS* AT ONCE IS SOMETHING *I* CAN'T DO.

4

THEN WHAT IN BLAZES ARE YA *DOIN'* THIS FOR?

I KNOW WHY *I'M* IN IT. ALL THOSE SUPER-HERO *GROUPIES* OUT THERE.

WHAT A WAY TO SPEND A *CAREER.*

Y'KNOW, I NEVER *INTENDED* TO BE A HERO -- IT WAS AN *ACCIDENT.*

"I WAS VISITING MY UNCLE'S *LABORATORY* WHEN *LIGHTNING* SHATTERED HIS CHEMICALS.

"THEY SPILLED OVER ME-- *CHANGED* ME... I FOUND THAT I WAS GIVEN SUPER-SPEED... LIKE *THE FLASH* HIMSELF.

"AT FIRST I WORE A *COSTUME* LIKE HIS -- THEN I GOT MY *OWN* UNIFORM.

"IN THE BEGIN- NING, I LOVED IT. BUT NOW... I DON'T KNOW."

MAYBE I'M NOT *CUT OUT* FOR THE SUPER-HERO GAME.

MAYBE THIS ISN'T THE TIME TO *TELL* YOU, BUT WHEN WE LAND, I'LL BE *TAKING OFF.*

I'VE GOT MY *OWN* WORK-- WITH THE *DRUG CENTERS.*

THAT'S MY *REAL* JOB. FIGHTING SUPER-VILLAINS IS JUST *FUN*--IN A *PER-VERTED* SORT OF WAY.

I'LL *MISS* YOU, SPEEDY. YOU'RE REALLY VERY *NICE.*

NICE, SHMICE! WHO CARES ABOUT *HIM* LEAVING?

WANNA KNOW WHAT *REALLY* BUGS ME?

IT'S THIS *SPEEDY! ROBIN! STARFIRE! GARBAGE!*

I THOUGHT I'M *ONE* OF YA. WHEN ARE YA GONNA TELL ME YOUR *REAL* NAMES?

WHEN YOU'RE *READY,* SQUIRT.

YEAH? I BET YOU TOLD *EACH OTHER* WHEN YOU FIRST MET.

MAYBE THAT WAS A *MISTAKE.*

LISTEN, OIL-BREATH...

5

I'M REALLY STARTING TO WONDER.

I'M GOING TO MISS YOU, FRAN.

YOU DON'T HAVE TO. YOU CAN STILL COME WITH ME.

WELL, I GUESS THIS IS IT. WHOSE GONNA BE THE FIRST TO KISS ME GOOD-BYE?

AND I DON'T MEAN YOU, LOGAN.

NO TAKERS? WELL, THEN IT'S UP TO ME.

COME HERE, YOU TAWNY VIXEN!

MMFMM FFMMF MM

SKREEEE!

WHAT IN THE WORLD--?!?

THIS IS PRICELESS. SOMEONE, GET ME A POLAROID.

OOPS. I'M SORRY. YOU TOOK ME BY SURPRISE.

DON'T APOLOGIZE, HONEY. I ALWAYS WANTED TO DO THAT TO HIM MYSELF.

NOW Y' WANNA TRY THAT WITH ME?

UHH, NO, THANKS, TERRA. I THINK I'LL JUST SAY MY GOOD-BYES.

OKAY, EVERYONE-- THAT'S IT. LET'S GET OUT OF HERE.

WE'VE ALL GOT REAL LIVES TO LIVE.

7

SAINT LOUIS...

GET *BACK*, ALL OF YOU.

WE CAN'T CONTROL OURSELVES MUCH LONGER.

MY BROTHER IS *RIGHT.* PROVOKE US AND YOU WILL *SUFFER.*

SIR? WHAT DO WE DO?

YOU SAW WHAT THEY DID TO THAT *APARTMENT BUILDING.*

YOU EVER PLAY *POKER?* THERE'S *TWO* OF THEM AGAINST ONE HUNDRED OF US.

I THINK WE CAN PULL OFF A SUCCESS- FUL *BLUFF.*

GENTLEMEN, I SUGGEST YOU *SURRENDER* NOW OR WE WILL BE FORCED TO *OPEN FIRE!*

THAT'S A *MISTAKE,* GENERAL!

YOUR *LAST* MISTAKE.

YOU WILL LEARN HOW POWERFUL ARE *THUNDER* AND *LIGHTNING!*

THE SKY GROWS THICK AND BLACK AS THE NIGHT AS ELECTRICITY SPLITS THE DEEPENING DARK...

THEN COMES THE CLARION CALL OF DEATH ITSELF-- THE HEAVENS ROAR AS THUNDER BELLOWS WITH ANGER...

THOUGH NONE DIE, AT THIS MOMENT ALL WISH THEY HAD.

8

113

THE WINTER SKIES OVER NEW YORK CITY ARE GRAY AND BLEAK, OFFERING LITTLE HOPE TO THOSE WHO VENTURE OUT...

BETTER TO STAY INSIDE, OR AT LEAST THAT'S WHAT *VICTOR STONE* BELIEVES...

WHAT ARE *YOU* DOING HERE, PAL? THE *RATS* FORCE YOU OUTTA YOUR PLACE?

NAH. JUST THOUGHT I'D TAKE IT *EASY,* CATCH ON SOME *READING.* WHAT'S *UP?*

TARA AND ME ARE GOING TO A MOVIE.

"FRIDAY THE THIRTEENTH, PART THIRTEEN." *EVERYONE* DIES IN THIS ONE.

WANNA *COME?*

NAH. I THINK I'LL WAIT FOR THE NEW *STAR WARS* PIC INSTEAD.

I THINK YOU'RE RIGHT, DONNA-- I'M NOT GOING TO *BOTHER* WITH DICK ANY MORE.

GOOD FOR YOU. IF HE *REALLY* CARES, HE'LL LET YOU KNOW.

YOU *AGREE,* RAVEN?

I ...I DO NOT *KNOW.* I AM ILL AT EASE WITH *SOCIAL PROTOCOL.*

BUT I'M STILL *WORRIED* ABOUT HIM.

I KNOW, BUT WE'VE *ALL* ASKED HIM WHAT'S WRONG AND HE WON'T *TELL.*

WE CAN'T KEEP *CHASING* HIM. IT'S UP TO *HIM* NOW.

THE EMERGENCY ALARM SIGNALS IN EVERY ROOM, AND...

SOME-THING *WRONG* SPEEDY?

YEAH. I THINK YOU'LL WANNA *HEAR* THIS.

THERE'S SOMETHING ON THE *WIRE-SERVICE* YOU SHOULD KNOW ABOUT.

SOME KINDA *SUPER-BADDIE* TROUBLE DOWN IN ST. LOUIS.

THANKS. WE'LL PICK YOU UP ON OUR WAY *DOWN.*

SORRY, GORGEOUS, BUT NO CAN *DO.*

I'M ON A *SPECIAL ASSIGNMENT* DOWN IN WASHINGTON -- SO, GOOD LUCK, GUYS.

LEMME *KNOW* HOW IT PANS OUT.

9

WELL, YOU *WANTED* TO BE A TITAN.

I ALSO WANTED TO SEE A *MOVIE.* GUESS WHICH *WINS?*

RAYEN, YOU LOOK SO SAD. CAN I *HELP* YOU?

I DO NOT *THINK* SO, STARFIRE. BUT THANK YOU.

REALLY, I *WANT* TO HELP.

I KNOW WE'RE *DIFFERENT.* MY BACKGROUND *JUSTIFIES* VIOLENCE, YOURS *SHUNS* IT AT ALL COSTS--

--AND I KNOW WE HAVEN'T BEEN ALL THAT *CLOSE...*

...BUT I REALLY DO *LIKE* YOU.

AND I KNOW YOU'VE BEEN *HURT...*

KORIAND'R...STARFIRE... WHAT I *AM* IS WHAT HURTS ME. THERE CAN BE NO *SIMPLE SOLUTION.*

...DON'T KNOW WHERE *DICK* RAN OFF TO...SO I GUESS THAT LEAVES *YOU* IN CHARGE.

ME? WHY NOT *YOU?*

I *HATE* THIS, LOGAN.

DON'T WE HAVE A DAY OFF?

'CAUSE THE WAY I'VE BEEN FEELIN' LATELY, I'D MARCH US RIGHT INTO A *DEATH TRAP.*

WHAT'S *UP?*

I MET SARAH'S *FIANCE.* ANY LAWS AGAINST ME *SQUEEZIN'* HIM-- *REAL HARD?*

AT LEAST ONE OR TWO.

I'M SORRY TO *HEAR* ABOUT THAT, VIC. NOW I UNDER-STAND WHY YOU SOUNDED SO *STRANGE* WHEN I MENTIONED TERRY'S PROPOSAL.

SO YOU *ARE* MARRYIN' 'IM?

I--I *WANT* TO. BUT I HAVEN'T SAID *YES* YET.

STRANGE, ISN'T IT? I DON'T FLINCH AT TAKING ON CREEPS LIKE *BROTHER BLOOD*--

--BUT WHEN IT COMES TO MARCHING DOWN THE AISLE, I *FREEZE.*

10

DON'T YOU UNDERSTAND US YET?

SEND A *THOUSAND* SOLDIERS AGAINST US AND IT *STILL* WON'T MATTER.

TAVIS, IT IS BECOMING IMPOSSIBLE TO *RESTRAIN* MYSELF.

DO SOMETHING BEFORE IT IS TOO LATE.

WE WANT *HIM!* FIND HIM FOR US OR ELSE!

SORRY, BOYS, BUT I THINK YOU'VE WAITED *TOO LONG.*

MAYBE THE *MILITARY* CAN'T STOP YOU, BUT THEY *CAN!*

I *SEE* THEM. LET'S GO!

YOU'RE THE *TITANS?* I THOUGHT THE *JUSTICE LEAGUE* WAS COMING.

DON'T WORRY, WE'LL DO JUST *FINE.*

THEY'RE THE PROBLEM?

BET YOUR SWEET-- UH, YEAH, THEY'RE *IT!* THEY CALL THEMSELVES *THUNDER AND LIGHTNING.*

THEY'RE NOT *GOING* ANYWHERE, WONDER GIRL. I'VE *GOT* THEM.

I *AGREE* WITH YOU, BROTHER... WE CAN WAIT *NO LONGER.*

GOOD! THE ENERGIES THAT FLOW THROUGH ME ARE *READY* TO EXPLODE!

I MUST *RELEASE* THEM.

11

ASK? YOU HAVEN'T ASKED FOR ANYTHING. YOU'VE DEMANDED, YOU'VE DESTROYED.

IT AIN'T WORKIN' WONDY... FORGET 'BOUT TALKING.

CYBORG'S RIGHT-- WE OUTNUMBER THEM!

LET'S JUST STOP THEM!

NO!

MY GOD, I'M FALLING! GAR?!?

I SEE YA. HOLD ON WHILE I CHANGE INTO ANOTHER SHAPE AN' CATCH YA.

DON'T BOTHER, CHANGELING-- I'LL LOWER TERRA WITH A SUPER-SPEED CUSHION OF AIR.

OUGHT TO DO SOMETHING BEFORE I ANNOUNCE MY DECISION!

GET BACK. I WARN YOU-- STAY AWAY FROM US!

NO WAY, PALLIE-- I'M COMIN' FOR YA!

AN' NOT YOU OR THIS MAKESHIFT LIGHTNING'S GONNA STOP ME!

BATHOOOM!

NOT GOOD... I'VE GOT A FEELING THEY DON'T WANT TO FIGHT-- BUT AS LONG AS THEY WON'T LISTEN TO REASON...

THOOM!

...WE'VE GOT NO CHOICE.

13

IT'S LIKE TRYING TO MOVE A 747... BUT IF I KEEP APPLYING *CONSTANT PRESSURE,* HE'LL GIVE IN.

AS STRONG AS THUNDER IS, I'M *STRONGER...*

WONDER GIRL-- *DON'T!* I SENSE HIS *POWER* BUILDING.

LEAVE-- LEAVE HIM!

YOU *HEARD* HER... MOVE AWAY OR YOU'RE *DEAD!*

NO. WE TALK!

KRASH!

NO! I AM *THROUGH* TALKING. WE HAVE WASTED *YEARS* TALKING...

IT IS NOW TIME FOR *ACTION!*

FOOM!

SO ACTION IT *IS.*

HE WASN'T *EXPECTING* THAT... I THINK I CAN KEEP HIM *OFF-BALANCE* ... MOVE SO FAST HE'LL NEVER *TOUCH* ME.

UH-OH-- *VIC!* BEHIND YOU!

THANKS, BUT MY *INTERNAL AMPLIFIERS* ALREADY TOLD ME HE WAS *SKULKING* THERE.

HAD PLENTY A' TIME TO GET MY *WHITE SOUND BLASTER* IN PLACE.

WE *WARNED* YOU... WE *PLEADED* WITH YOU.

BUT NO MORE. NOW WE FIGHT TO *KILL.*

YEAH, YEAH, THAT'S WHAT THEY *ALL* SAY.

GOD, YOU'D THINK YOU *JERKS* COULD COME UP WITH *SNAPPIER DIALOGUE.*

WHY DON'TCHA GET YERSELF A *JOKE-WRITER* ...LIKE ME.

14

BE CAREFUL, GAN... HE MOVES TOO SWIFTLY TO TOUCH.

I KNOW THAT, TAVIS, AND I AM PREPARED.

COME, FAST ONE -- I AM NOT DONE WITH YOU.

YOU MAY AS WELL BE, JERKO...

...CAUSE YOU'RE NOT GETTIN' THE CHANCE TO DO ANYTHING ELSE.

TERRA?!?

SHOOOM!

IN THE COSTUME, FLEET-FEET. NOT BAD, AM I?

BLAM!

ACHH!

LOGAN -- THE LIGHTNING GOT 'IM!...

CYBORG, HOW IS HE?

SKREEEE

BREATHING, THANK GOD...GET THE WITCH OVER HERE. HE NEEDS HER.

GAN, HELP ME!

TAVIS?

THE FEMALE'S BLAST... IT HURTS...HURTS BADLY...PLEASE HELP ME.

THAT IS IT. THE BATTLE IS OVER.

MY BROTHER NEEDS ME.

IT'S ABOUT TIME. NO ONE HAS TO DIE.

15

DIE? WE WILL *BOTH* DIE IF WE DO NOT FIND SECOND LIEUTENANT WALTER WILLIAMS.

YOU STILL HAVEN'T TOLD US-- *WHY* DO YOU WANT HIM?

IS THAT *IMPORTANT,* WONDER GIRL? THE BOY IS BADLY *HURT.*

QUESTIONS CAN WAIT FOR LATER. LET ME *HELP...*

DON'T, RAVEN -- WITH YOUR *POWERS* THE WAY THEY'VE BEEN, YOU CAN'T TAKE THE *CHANCE.*

BUT HOW CAN I *IGNORE* HIM? I AM AN *EMPATH.* I MUST--

YOU CAN'T, RAVEN -- NOT NOW... NOT UNTIL WE *KNOW* WHY YOU HAVEN'T BEEN ABLE TO CONTROL YOURSELF.

GAN... IT IS... ALL RIGHT... I WAS ONLY *STUNNED.*

I... FEEL MY STRENGTH *RETURN.*

YOUR BROTHER WILL BE ALL RIGHT. I *KNOW* HE WILL.

THEN YOU DON'T KNOW WHAT YOU'RE TALKING ABOUT. HE'S *DYING...* JUST AS I AM.

IT BEGAN AT THE *BEGINNING* OF THE VIETNAMESE WAR. YOUR COUNTRY SENT "ADVISORS" TO MINE. ONE OF THOSE "ADVISORS" MET A NATIVE WOMAN.

THEY FELL IN LOVE AND FOR SEVERAL MONTHS THEY THOUGHT THEY WOULD NEVER PART. BUT THEN HE WAS ASSIGNED ELSEWHERE...

AND THEY *NEVER SAW* EACH OTHER AGAIN.

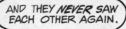

16

121

"THE WOMAN WAS *OSTRACIZED* FOR CARRYING HIS CHILD, AND WAS SENT FROM HER VILLAGE FOR THIS *CRIME*. IN TEARS SHE *LEFT* VIETNAM, BUT WHEREVER SHE WENT, SHE WAS REFUSED. THEN SHE FOUND THE FABLED LAND OF *HSUAN* IN THE NORTH CHINA SEA...

"HSUAN, WHERE ONCE THE DEAD WAS RETURNED TO LIFE. HSUAN, THOUGHT A MYTH BUT WAS REALITY. A PHANTOM ISLE WHERE THIS BANISHED WOMAN GAVE BIRTH TO SIAMESE TWINS...

"CHAN TI WAS A WISE MAN WHO SOME SAY WAS DESCENDED FROM THE GREAT *EMPEROR WU TI* HIMSELF. HE PERFORMED HIS CEREMONIES AND APPLIED THE JADE HERBS AND ANCIENT INCENSE.

"THE CHILDREN WERE *SEPARATED*... AS IF BY MAGIC, BUT ALL SENSED THEY WERE *DIFFERENT*. ONE COULD CALL UPON THE *THUNDER*--AND THE OTHER COULD WIELD THE VERY *LIGHTNING* ITSELF.

WE ARE THOSE CHILDREN, BORN OF *AMERICAN* BLOOD MINGLED WITH *VIETNAMESE.*

AND NOW WE SEARCH FOR SECOND LIEUTENANT WALTER WILLIAMS -- *OUR FATHER.*

THERE ARE TIMES WHEN OUR POWERS CANNOT BE *CONTROLLED.* AT THESE TIMES OUR PAIN IS *GREAT.*

CHAN TI SAYS WE NEED OUR FATHER -- HIS *BLOOD* IS OUR ONLY SALVATION.

WE ASKED YOUR GOVERNMENT, BUT THEY SAY THERE IS NO *RECORD* OF A SECOND LIEUTENANT WALTER WILLIAMS.

THEY WILL NOT *HELP,* AND TIME IS GROWING *SHORT.*

OH, WOW.

THERE'S GOT TO BE SOME *MISTAKE.*

WE'LL *HELP* THEM, WON'T WE?

WE'LL DO WHAT WE *CAN.*

I KNOW SOMEONE IN *ARMY INTELLIGENCE.* SHE'LL GET US THE INFORMATION.

YOU DON'T *NEED* TO. WE HAVE A *COMPUTER READ-OUT* ... WILLIAMS' LAST KNOWN ADDRESS IN A FISHING VILLAGE IN *MAINE,* BUT...

WE CANNOT *WAIT.*

NOW, TAVIS... LET US *GO!*

WAIT!

STOP THEM! WILLIAMS HAS A SPECIAL GOVERNMENT CODE -- YOU WON'T *FIND* HIM.

18

THEY WON'T GET AWAY, I'LL FOLLOW THEM.

DON'T BOTHER, STARFIRE. WE KNOW WHERE THEY'RE GOING.

RAVEN-- I WILL MEET YOU AT THE VILLAGE AND I WILL TRY TO KEEP THINGS PEACEFUL UNTIL YOU ARRIVE.

LET'S JUST HOPE YOU CAN.

OKAY, WHAT DO WE DO NOW? FOLLOW THEM AND START ANOTHER FIGHT?

WHAT DO YOU MEAN?

THEY'RE IN TROUBLE. CAN'T WE HELP?

I THINK SO.

AND I HAVE AN IDEA. LISTEN...

MAINE...

...ON A NIGHT WHEN NONE SHOULD STRAY FROM HOME.

FAITH!

19

THE SKY EXPLODES WITH THUNDER'S SCREAM AND LIGHTNING'S CALL...

AND EVEN A WEATHER-WEARY VILLAGE KNOWS WHEN THINGS ARE NOT AS THEY SHOULD BE.

THEY'RE AFRAID, EVERYONE HERE... AND THEIR FEARS ARE, AS EVER, PAINFUL.

YET, I CAN 'FEEL' IT... EVEN ABOVE ALL THESE OTHERS.

I FEEL THEIR PAIN!

WHERE IS HE? WHERE IS OUR FATHER?!?

PLEASE STOP... DO NOT DO THIS. I UNDERSTAND YOUR PAINS... I UNDERSTAND YOU.

IF YOU CONTINUE LIKE THIS, YOU WILL NOT BE ABLE TO STOP!

YOU CAN'T UNDERSTAND, WE NEED OUR FATHER.

SPAK

AND YOUR GOVERNMENT WON'T KEEP US FROM HIM.

NO ONE WILL KEEP US FROM FINDING HIM.

20

TAVIS, ARE YOU *ALL* RIGHT?

I... AM, MY *LEGS* HURT... MY *ARMS* ARE IN PAIN. PERHAPS WE SHOULD *CEASE* ALL FIGHTING.

NO! WE MUSTN'T. THEY WON'T HELP US.

WE WILL *NEVER* BE DEFEATED.

YOU'RE *WRONG,* GRANITE-BREATH!

FIRST FLOOR, LADIES LINGERIE, MEN'S CLOTHES AND JANITOR-IN-A-DRUM, GOING *DOWWNNN.*

WHOMP!

SPAK!

PAL...

SPOOM!

...THAT WAS A *BIG* MISTAKE!

FLASHER! PITCH COMIN' TO *FIRST!*

GOT 'IM, CYBORG, HE'S SPINNING OUT... GOING... GOING... GOING...

ISN'T HE *GONE* YET?

YOU WANT ME TO SET HIM FREE?

ON SECOND THOUGHT...

22

WE SHOULD RETURN HOME... IF WE ARE TO DIE...

NO, DON'T *THINK* THAT, GAN... THERE'S ALWAYS *HOPE.*

HE'S RIGHT... WE CAN CHECK *S.T.A.R.* LABS...

MAYBE THE SCIENTISTS *THERE* CAN HELP.

AT LEAST IT'S WORTH A *TRY.*

AND LATER...

WHAT A *SHAME.* IF ONLY THEIR FATHER HADN'T *DIED.*

HE *DIDN'T,* STARFIRE. I NEVER SAID HE *DID.*

BUT YOU SAID...

THEY NEVER WOULD HAVE STOPPED THEIR DESTRUCTIVE WAVE IF THEY THOUGHT HE WAS *ALIVE.*

HE WAS A *MILITARY SCIENTIST* IN VIETNAM, BUT FOR SOME REASON EVERYTHING WENT *WRONG* FOR HIM. ONE DAY HE *DISAPPEARED...*

...FLEW TO *AMERICA.* AND HE'S BEEN WANTED BY THE GOVERNMENT EVER SINCE THE '60'S...

...BUT NOT EVEN MY SISTER, WITH HER *ACCESS* TO PENTAGON COMPUTERS, COULD FIND OUT *WHAT* HE DID, *WHY* HE RAN OR, MORE IMPORTANTLY-- *WHERE* HE IS NOW.

HE'S BEEN DECLARED *TOP SECRET...* SOMETHING'S *WRONG* HERE, GUYS... SOMETHING'S *VERY WRONG.*

AND WE'RE GOING TO HAVE TO FIND OUT *WHAT!*

129

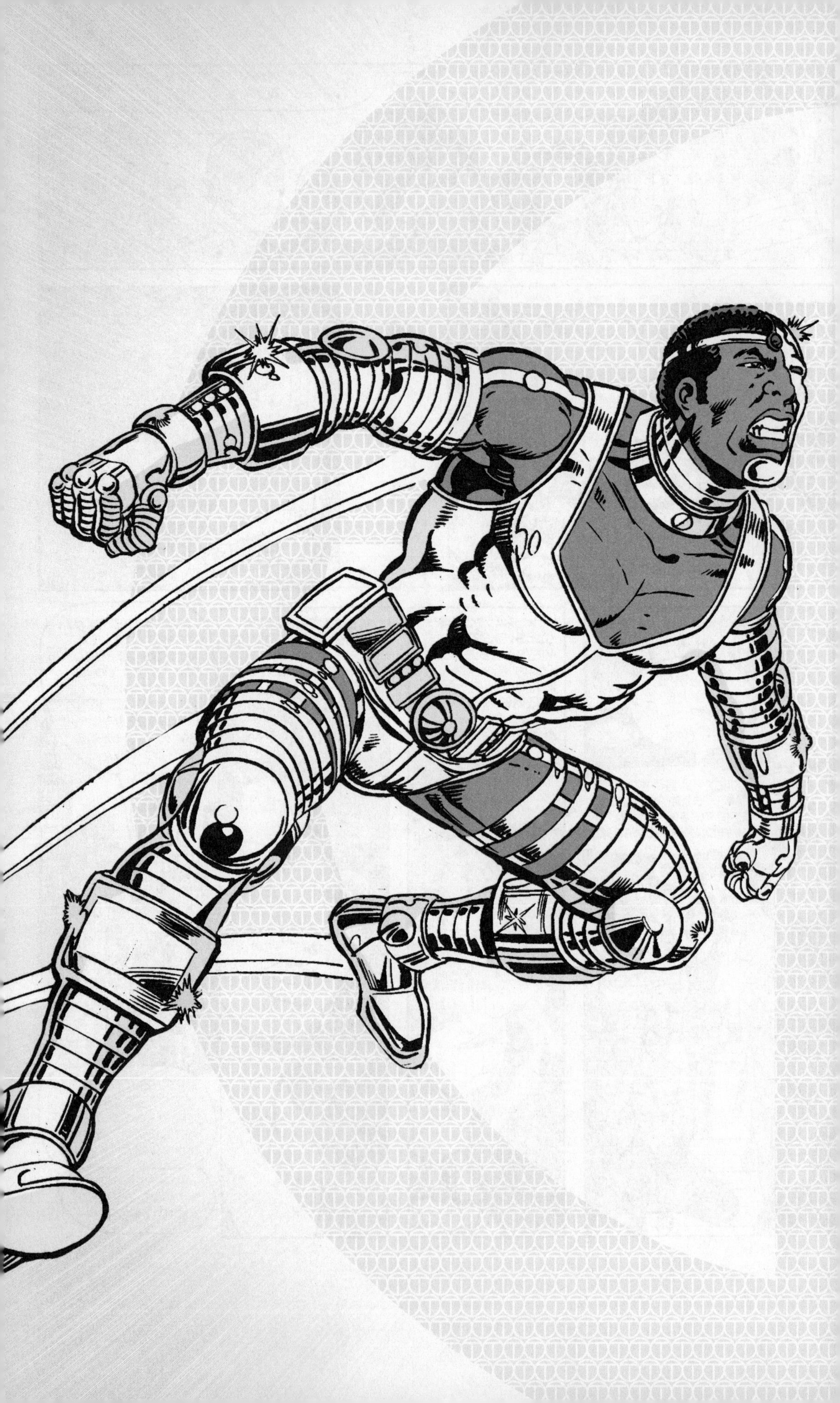

YOU KNOW I LOVE OCCASIONALLY *JOINING* YOU ON A TITANS' CASE, BUT NEXT TIME--

--GIVE ME A LESS *GRISLY* TASK.

SORRY, I HOPE OUR NEXT *MURDER CASE* WILL BE PRETTIER.

I DON'T UNDERSTAND. WHO COULD HAVE KILLED *HIM* WITH HIS OWN *WEAPON?*

GOOD QUESTION, STARFIRE. I THOUGHT WE WERE GETTING A *LEAD* ON TRIDENT, THEN *THIS* HAPPENS.

FRANKLY, I'M *STUMPED.*

WE'LL RUN A *MAKE* ON HIM DOWNTOWN, BUT DO YOU *RECOGNIZE* HIM, MISS?

SORRY. STRANGE, I DIDN'T *PICTURE* HIM LOOKING LIKE THAT.

HE SEEMED SO *SOFT* WHEN WE FOUGHT.

SOFT? FORGET IT, WONDER *GIRL*. HE'S *SOLID MUSCLE.*

LISTEN, WE CAN'T DO ANYTHING MORE *HERE.* LET'S CHECK HIM OUT ON THE *COMPUTERS* BACK IN THE TOWER.

WHICH IS THE *PERFECT* TIME FOR ME TO SAY "SO LONG."

YOU KNOW IT. DUTIES IN *ATLANTIS* AWAIT... ALSO THIS *GORGEOUS* YOUNG MERMAID TYPE.

TAKE CARE, AQUALAD-- AND *THANKS.*

SEEYA, PALS.

YOU'VE GOT TO GO *ALREADY?*

②

ON A PRIVATE ISLAND LOCATED IN MANHATTAN'S EAST RIVER...

WELL, WHATTAYA THINK? YOU LIKE IT?

IT'S BEAUTIFUL, VIC. HOW DID YOU DO IT?

HOLOGRAPHICS. WE CAN SET THE COMPUTER TO SIMULATE ANY BACKGROUND.

YOU WANT THE ARCTIC? PARIS? YOU NAME IT, YOU GOT IT!

IT'S LOVELY AS IT IS, BUT I CAN'T THINK ABOUT HOLOGRAMS RIGHT NOW.

I STILL WANT TO KNOW WHO KILLED TRIDENT.

FORGET IT. HE'S DEAD. SO WE SCRATCH ONE SUPER-VILLAIN.

WHAT'S THE DIFFERENCE?

THE DIFFERENCE, FLASHER, IS WE GOT A MURDERER FREE OUT THERE.

SO, LIKE FLEET-FEET SAYS -- WHO CARES?

SAVES US THE PROBLEM.

TERRA, WE WOULD NOT HAVE KILLED HIM.

GREAT! WE'VE GOT A MYSTERY AND ROBBIE'S GONE. HE'D FIGGER THIS OUT IN A SEC.

WELL, HE AIN'T HERE, SALAD-HEAD -- SO IT'S UP TO US.

YEAH, AND SINCE WE SAW HIM FIRST, I'LL BEGIN.

BUT, BEFORE GAR LOGAN SPEAKS, VICTOR STONE REMEMBERS...

3

WHY DIDN'T YOU *SPEAK* TO SARAH WHEN SHE CALLED?

LOGAN, MIND YER OWN *BUSINESS.*

C'MON, VIC-- WE'RE *FRIENDS...*

LOOK, *I DON'T* WANNA SPEAK TO HER. SHE'S GOT HER LIFE, I GOT MINE. SO *BUTT OUT!*

MEMORIES COME TO AN *ABRUPT* END AS...

SO WHATTAYA *WAITIN'* FOR, GREENIE? START TALKING. JUST DON'T *BORE* US.

"*BORE YOU?*" OKAY, LADY, YOU *ASKED* FOR THIS.

♪ TA DA DA DA DA DADADADA... ♫

I ASKED FOR A *STORY,* SO WHATTA I GET? "*JAWS 3-D!*"

STAND BACK, EVERYONE. THIS ONE'S ON *ME!*

WOP!

YAGHHH!

MY NOSE! MY BEAUTIFUL NOSE!

YOU *BROKE* IT! I'LL *SUE* YOU FOR EVERY CENT YOU'VE GOT.

GO RIGHT AHEAD, BOZO-BREATH. YOU STILL WON'T HAVE *CHANGE* FOR A DIME!

WONDY, IS IT AGAINST TITANS' BY-LAWS TO *KILL* A NEW MEMBER?

OKAY, OKAY, I'M *SORRY.*

PLEASE DON'T THROW ME OUTTA THE GROUP... PLEASE.

DON'T WORRY, TARA -- WE'VE *ALL* WANTED TO BOP LOGAN.

NOW, IF HE WON'T MIND *STARTING* HIS STORY...

④

YEAH, YEAH, OKAY, IT BEGAN WHEN I WAS *VISITIN'* WHAT'S-HIS-JUNKPILE OVER THERE...

...TRYIN' TO *EXPLAIN* TO HIM THE "*GREEN EXPERIENCE!*"

"THAT'S WHEN EVERYTHING WENT *KABLOOEY!*"

SKROOOOM!

WHAT IN THE *WORLD?* YOU *HEAR* THAT?

NO. I'M COMPLETELY *DEAF!* OF COURSE I HEARD IT, YOU *JERK.*

AN *EXPLOSION...* SOMEPLACE *UPTOWN!*

"WELL, IT DIDN'T TAKE LONG FOR ME TO FLY THERE WHILE SALVAGE-SIDES *LEAPED* UP TO THE EIGHTIES, WHERE..."

IF YA *VALUE* YER LIVES-- *STAY BACK* WHILE I *SPLIT!*

THEN NO ONE ELSE GETS *HURTS!*

WELL, LOOKEE HERE, RUSTHEAD-- A JERK WITH AN OVERSIZED *COCKTAIL FORK!*

TITANS?

I WAS *WONDERIN'* IF EITHER YOU CREEPS OR THAT *FIREHEAD* CHARACTER WOULD SHOW UP TO STOP ME.

Y'SEE, I'VE BEEN *ITCHIN'* TA TRY OUT THIS *GIZMO!*

FOOOSHH

"*ITCHING?*" THEN YOU'VE UNSIGHTLY *DRY SCALP...* PROBABLY A SIGN OF *DANDRUFF!*

YOU REALLY OUGHTTA TRY THAT *SHAMPOO,* THEN MAYBE THAT CUTE *SECRETARY* IN THE ELEVATOR WILL NOTICE YA.

5

FACT IS, YOU AIN'T EVEN SAVED YERSELF!

SKROOOOMM!

HE'S BLASTED THE GIRDERS ...THEY'RE *FALLIN'*!

NO TIME TO MOVE... AND GAR'S STILL *OUT* OF IT...

GOTTA HOPE DAD MADE THIS BODY STRONG ENOUGH TO *WITHSTAND* THAT SORT'A WEIGHT SMASHIN' ONTO IT.

"VIC SPUN HIS MOLYBDENUM STEEL-PLATED BODY, PROTECTING YOURS TRULY FROM A TON OF ALMOST CERTAIN DEATH..."

KEEP STILL, LOGAN -- AN' CROSS YOUR *FINGERS*!

I-I HEARD VIC CRY OUT. EVEN IF HIS HEAD *IS* AS THICK AS HIS BODY, IT STILL HURT.

BUT HE *SAVED* ME ANYWAY.

WHAT *ELSE* COULD I DO? HE STILL OWED ME *FIVE BUCKS.*

ONLY *TRIDENT* GOT AWAY WITH MORE THAN $125,000.

ANYONE SEE *STARFIRE*?

YEAH, SHE WENT TO LOCATE *DICK.*

SHE FIGURED THIS CASE WAS UP *HIS* ALLEY.

7

PRINCESS KORIAND'R OF TAMARAN HURTLES THROUGH THE EVENING SKY, THE COLD INVIGORATING HER, THOUGH IT HARDLY ERASES THE WORRY SHE FEELS...

SOMETHING HAS BEEN BOTHERING THE MAN SHE LOVES, SOMETHING HE WON'T TALK ABOUT...

JUST OUTSIDE GOTHAM CITY...

WAYNE

...AT STATELY WAYNE MANOR...

MASTER JASON, ANSWERING THE DOORBELL IS MY JOB.

SO? WITH BRUCE AWAY, IT'S BORING HERE, LET ME DO--

--SOMETHING??

OBOY.

HI, I--UH...

UHHHHH...

AND NOW SHE'LL GET HER ANSWERS...

MISS STARFIRE, PLEASE, COME IN...

IS IT ALL RIGHT, ALFRED?

YES, YOUNG JASON TODD KNOWS MASTER BRUCE'S SECRET.

I CAME TO SEE DICK.

BUT HE MOVED OUT WHEN MASTER BRUCE TOOK ON MASTER JASON AS HIS NEW WARD.

DICK'S MOVED OUT? HE DIDN'T TELL THE TITANS.

I'VE GOT TO FIND HIM.

THANKS, ALFRED. AND NICE MEETING YOU, JASON. 'BYE.

SIGHHH! AM I TOO YOUNG TO BE A TITAN, TOO?

8

ANYONE FOR *HOT CHOCOLATE?*

HEY, GUACOMOLE-BREATH, MAKE ME A *DOUBLE.*

SURE, AS LONG AS I WAS ASKED SO *SWEETLY.*

... THAT ALL HAPPENED YESTERDAY *MORNING.* RAVEN AND I FOUGHT HIM IN THE *AFTERNOON.*

AN' FLEET-FEET AND I TRASHED 'IM THAT *NIGHT,* WHILE HE WAS *SNEEZING* LIKE THAT STUPID *DISNEY DWARF.*

VIC, ARE YOU *SURE* HE STOLE A HUNDRED THOU? I DIDN'T GET THAT *IMPRESSION* FROM HIM.

FRANKLY, I FOUND HIM *CONFUSED...UNCERTAIN.*

NO, WALLACE, I SENSED HE WAS *CUNNING...* AND QUITE *SHREWD...*

"FOR *US,* IT BEGAN WHEN WONDER GIRL ASKED ME TO WALK WITH HER..."

YOU'VE HAD *SEVERAL* ATTACKS LATELY -- FOR YOUR OWN SAKE, RAVEN, LET US *HELP* YOU.

ON PARADISE ISLAND WE HAVE CERTAIN *MACHINES...*

I AM SORRY, BUT THEY CANNOT *CHANGE* WHAT I AM.

I AM *TRIGON'S* CHILD, AND ONE WAY OR ANOTHER THAT *DEVIL* INTENDS TO POSSESS ME.

RAVEN, PLEASE -- YOU CAN'T CONTINUE TO BE *TORTURED* LIKE YOU'VE BEEN. TRUST US, WE'RE YOUR *FRIENDS.*

"WE WALKED THROUGH THE MUSEUM OF NATURAL HISTORY AND I WAS FASCINATED BY THE EXHIBITS. BUT THEN..."

GET *OUTTA* HERE. *RUN!*

THERE'S A *CRAZY GUY* IN THERE!

FOR GOD'S SAKE -- DON'T *PANIC.*

9

DO A QUICK *SCAN* OF THE PLACE...

I'VE GOT A HUNCH THIS COULD BE THE *SAME GUY* CYBORG AND CHANGELING FOUGHT.

LET US *HOPE.* WITH OUR POWERS, HE CANNOT *ESCAPE.*

WHAT?

I SAW THE *LOOK* IN HER EYES... SHE IS *WORRIED* ABOUT ME. BUT THERE WAS NO NEED FOR *CONCERN.*

I *CONTROL* MY ACTIONS. I AM IN *FULL COMMAND* OF MY POWERS.

YES, THERE HE IS -- AS VICTOR AND GARFIELD *DESCRIBED.*

WHO? HMMM. I *RECOGNIZE* HER... SHE IS ONE OF THE *TEEN TITANS.* FASCINATING.

IF *ONE* IS ABOUT, THEN THERE MIGHT WELL BE *OTHERS.*

I CANNOT *DELAY.*

BE *CAREFUL,* GIRL -- PERMIT ME TO LEAVE IN PEACE OR SOMEONE WILL BE *HURT!*

SKROOOOMM!

YOU'RE RIGHT ABOUT *THAT,* TRIDENT--

WHAT?

10

--ONLY THAT SOMEONE IS GOING TO BE *YOU*!!

NO MATTER. THERE IS A SIMPLE WAY TO *DEAL* WITH YOU.

FOOOSH!

WONDER GIRL *TOO?* ARE THE *OTHERS* HERE AS WELL?

NOTE MY *TRIDENT*, A RATHER *INGENIOUS* DEVICE, WOULDN'T YOU SAY?

THE *CENTER* TINE SHALL CREATE ALL THE *DAMAGE* NEEDED TO DETAIN YOU.

NO! FIRE SPREADING EVERYWHERE...

MAYBE ALL THOSE YEARS LIVING ON PARADISE ISLAND MAKE ME MORE *AWARE* OF THEIR VALUE--

--BUT I SIMPLY *CAN'T* LET THOSE ANTIQUES BE *DAMAGED*,

MUCH BETTER. NOW I HAVE A CLEAR PATH *OUT* OF HERE...

UNHH! NERO'S TREASURES WEIGH ALMOST AS MUCH AS THE *MAN* DID HIMSELF!

THEN *RETURN* THEM, TRIDENT.

RETURN THEM BEFORE *HARM* BEFALLS YOU.

AGAIN? ALL RIGHT THEN, GIRL-- *COME*, TAKE ME CAPTIVE....

....*IF YOU CAN.*

11

PLEASE, DO NOT MAKE ME USE MY *POWERS*. I DO NOT KNOW IF THEY CAN BE *CONTROLLED*.

THAT DOESN'T *MATTER*, RAVEN, GO AHEAD-- TAKE ME *PRISONER*.

MY *HAND*?!? IT--

WENT *THROUGH* ME? PERHAPS... *FASCINATING*, ISN'T IT?

STILL, MY *TANGIBILITY* IS THE LEAST OF YOUR WORRIES.

YOUR *CLOAK*, RAVEN-- LOOK AT IT.

NO!

HURRY, GIRL, REMOVE IT BEFORE IT BECOMES YOUR *FUNERAL PYRE*.

HE'S *PLAYING* WITH US... WELL, I'LL GIVE HIM ALL THE *ROPE* HE WANTS, AND THEN GLADLY TIGHTEN THE *NOOSE*.

THIS IS TOO *SIMPLE*. HOW CAN YOU CATCH--

"-- WHAT IS NO LONGER THERE?"

GONE? BUT CYBORG DIDN'T SAY HE COULD TELEPORT.

BLAST! WHAT'S HE UP TO?

HEY, WHERE DID THAT GUY GO? HE JUST *VANISHED*?

DID YOU *SENSE* ANY THING *STRANGE* ABOUT HIM?

I--I DO NOT *KNOW*.

NOTHING... HE WAS AN *ORDINARY* MAN-- YET I CAN SAY *THIS*, WONDER GIRL--

MY HAND DID NOT GO *THROUGH* HIM. HE SIMPLY WAS *NOT* WHERE MY HAND TOUCHED.

12

HE *GOT AWAY*, SIMPLE AS THAT!

WHAT WAS *WRONG*, RAVEN? YOUR POWERS GO *CRAZY* AGAIN?

C'MON. BE FAIR. I COULDN'T STOP HIM, EITHER.

THE ONLY THING RAVE DID *WRONG* WAS MAKE HIM SOUND *TOO SMART*.

THAT GUY'S BRAIN WAS LEFT ON *SPIN-CYCLE*.

LOOK, AT LEAST *HE* COULD WALK AND CHEW GUM AT THE SAME TIME. CAN *YOU*?

I DID NOT *EXAGGERATE*, NOR COULD I HAVE *STOPPED* HIM.

HE POSSESSES GREAT ABILITIES AND UNDER-STANDS HOW BEST TO *USE* THEM.

SORRY, RAVEN, BUT FOR ONCE SALAD-HEAD'S *RIGHT*. TRIDENT EATS SOUP WITH A *FORK*.

Y'KNOW, *ROBBIE* WOULD FIGGER THIS ALL OUT IN *FIVE SECONDS*.

SO NATCH, THE *ONE* TIME WE NEED HIM, HE'S *OUT* SOMEWHERE. PROBABLY SAVING A *CAT*.

NOT *EXACTLY*. FOR AT THIS VERY MO-MENT ROBIN IS ON THE EASTERN TIP OF LONG ISLAND, WHERE...

I DON'T *UNDERSTAND*, CHASE. WE HAD ANTHONY SCARAPELLI CAUGHT RED-HANDED. HOW COULD HE BE *FREED*?

ASK ME SOMETHING I CAN *ANSWER*, KID. HE GOT TO SOMEONE WHO'S *SOFT* ON CRIME, OR ON HIS PAY-ROLL, OR A THOUSAND *OTHER* POSSIBILITIES.

BUT I'LL TELL YOU *THIS*, I HATE IT. I MAKE A TEXT-BOOK ARREST...

...BUT BECAUSE OF SOME STUPID *TECHNICALITY* A CREEP LIKE SCARAPELLI WHO PUSHES DRUGS TO KIDS GETS AWAY WITHOUT EVEN SPENDING A *NIGHT* BEHIND BARS.

ONLY, IF THE INFO I GOT TONIGHT PANS OUT, SCARAPELLI ISN'T *STAYING* FREE.

Y'KNOW, KID—SOMETIMES I *ENVY* YOU AN' THE BATMAN. YOU *DON'T* HAVE TO FOLLOW THE BOOK LIKE I DO.

WELL, YOU *READY*?

AS I'LL *EVER* BE.

LET'S GO.

13

WALL AHEAD. YOU GOT THAT THING?

ONE *BATARANG* COMING UP.

CLEAR SAILIN', KID.

NOW, STAY BACK, IT'S UP TO *ME*.

HE SLIPS AHEAD, CLUMSILY CRISS-CROSSING THE IMMACULATELY MANICURED GROUNDS...

THEN...

DON'T MOVE OR YER *DEAD*.

OKAY, OKAY, DON'T SHOOT. I *GIVE*.

WHO *ARE* YA? WHATTAYA *DOIN'* HERE?

JUST TAKING MY EVENING CONSTITUTIONAL. YOU DON'T *MIND*, DO YOU?

NAH, *I* DON'T THINK HE MINDS.

RIGHT?

WHAP!

YOU'RE NOT *HALF BAD*, KID.

TRUSS 'IM UP AN' LET'S GO.

14

MEANWHILE...

FLASHER, PUT A *HOLD* ON YOUR STORY. I DON'T WANNA *MISS* ANY OF IT WHILE I ANSWER THE PHONE.

RRINNGGG!

AND...

THAT WAS THE *POLICE*. THEY GOT A *MAKE* ON TRIDENT. HIS NAME'S *SAMMY JAYE*, KNOWN MUSCLE FOR THE *H.I.V.E.**

I WAS WONDERING WHY WE HAVEN'T *HEARD* FROM THOSE CREEPS IN A WHILE.

WHAT'S THE *H.I.V.E.?*

A CRIMINAL GANG RUN BY *SCIENTISTS*. THAT WOULD EXPLAIN HIS *TRIDENT* WEAPON.

*HIERARCHY FOR INTERNATIONAL VENGEANCE AND EXTERMINATION. --Len.

BUT *BANK ROBBERY* ISN'T TYPICAL *H.I.V.E.* BUSINESS. IT DOESN'T MAKE *SENSE*.

YOU SAID THEY WERE *CRIMINALS*. ISN'T THAT GOOD ENOUGH?

YOU HAVE A LOT TO *LEARN*, TARA. ORGANIZATIONS LIKE THE *H.I.V.E.* AREN'T INTERESTED IN *MONEY*. THEY WANT *POWER*.

HOLD ON, GUYS... I FOUND OUT SOMETHING ABOUT DI-- I MEAN, *ROBIN*.

CRIPES. HERE WE GO AGAIN, HIDIN' YOUR SECRET *ID'S* ON ME. I'M TELLIN' YA-- I *HATE* IT!

HE ISN'T AT HOME AND HE ISN'T REGISTERED IN ANY *COLLEGE DORMITORY*.

BUT LISTEN TO *THIS*...

15

DON'T WORRY, ROBIN CAN *HANDLE* HIMSELF!

I WOULDN'T BE SO SURE. YOU SEE THE WAY HE'S BEEN *ACTING* LATELY?

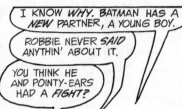

I KNOW *WHY.* BATMAN HAS A *NEW* PARTNER, A YOUNG BOY.

ROBBIE NEVER *SAID* ANYTHIN' ABOUT IT.

YOU THINK HE AND POINTY-EARS HAD A *FIGHT?*

LISSEN, NOBODY CARES ABOUT THAT. WE'VE GOT *TITANS* BUSINESS, SPEED-FREAK WAS GONNA TELL *OUR* STORY.

WITH MY PARENTS VACATIONING IN *BERMUDA,* I STUCK AROUND AFTER MOST OF YOU LEFT. THAT'S WHEN *TERRA* AND I HEARD TRIDENT HAD STRUCK *AGAIN* -- AT A JEWELRY STORE ON 83RD STREET.

WE HURRIED, BUT TRIDENT WAS *GONE.* WE FINALLY FOUND HIM UP BY THE *CROSS-BRONX EXPRESSWAY...*

SPEEDO, THIS SURE BEATS RIDIN' *ROCKS.* YOU THIS FAST WITH *EVERYTHING?*

WE'RE NOT HERE TO *CHIT-CHAT.* AND FRANKLY, I DIDN'T EVEN *WANT* YOU WITH ME.

I DON'T KNOW WHAT THE *OTHERS* THINK, BUT I DON'T BELIEVE *ANYTHING* YOU TOLD US.

OKAY, SO MAYBE I *STRETCHED* A POINT HERE OR THERE, BUT I WASN'T *LYING.*

YOU DON'T KNOW WHAT IT WAS LIKE-- DAD'S WIFE *HATED* ME AN' I COULDN'T STAY IN MARKOVIA.

THEN WHEN I WAS HELD BY THESE *TERRORISTS,* THEY KEPT ME DRUGGED SO I COULDN'T *ESCAPE.*

I USED TO GO TO BED *CRYING.* I-I WANTED TO KILL MYSELF BUT I WAS ALWAYS SO *SCARED.*

PLEASE, THIS IS MY *BIG CHANCE*--DON'T SAY ANYTHING THAT'LL GET ME THROWN OUTTA THE TITANS. PLEASE.

"TERRA AND I CHIT-CHATTED WHILE WE SEARCHED, THEN FINALLY FOUND HIM HIDING IN THAT BIG DRIVE-IN."

16

147

--BUT NOT GOOD ENUFF!

FOOOOSHH!

YEOWWWW!

SERVES ME RIGHT FOR NOT *THINKING* FIRST. WHERE'S MY *BRAINS?*

EVERYTHING'S FINALLY GOING MY WAY-- MUSTN'T BLOW IT *NOW!*

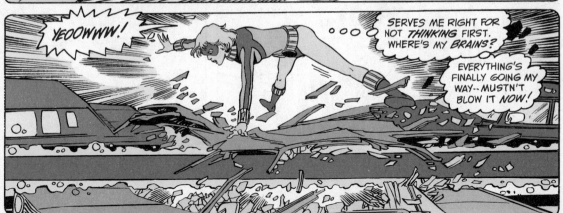

HAVE TO PUT ON *SPEED...* AND STOP HIM BEFORE HE TWISTS THAT *DIAL...*

KID FLASH!?!

WHA--?

WATCH OUT!

BLAST! I TURNED FOR A *SECOND,* BUT THAT'S ALL HE NEEDED TO SLICKEN THE PAVEMENT WITH *ICE.*

C-CAN'T GAIN TRACTION ...*SLIPPING...*

ACHHHH!

MAN, HOPE I DIDN'T *DISLOCATE* ANYTHING. ONLY MY SHOULDER HURTS... BAD.

THIS BROUHAHA HAS GONE ON *LONG ENOUGH.*

I'M TAKIN' OFF. SO YEW HAVE A *HOT TIME* IN THE OL' MOVIE TONIGHT, EH?

OH NO.

18

"I HAVE TO SAY THIS, TERRA THOUGHT FAST AND ACTED JUST AS QUICKLY...

"SHE BLEW OUT AN UNDERGROUND WATER MAIN WHICH PUT OUT THE FIRE BEFORE THERE WAS ANY PANIC.

WHATEVER I'VE THOUGHT OF HER IN THE PAST, SHE'S PROVED HERSELF.

UNFORTUNATELY, THOUGH, TRIDENT ESCAPED.

I DUNNO. DOESN'T SOUND LIKE THE GUY I FOUGHT.

SO WHAT'S THE PROBLEM?

LOOK, I DIDN'T FIGHT THIS TRIDENT, BUT IT SEEMS OBVIOUS TO ME--

--YOU ALL MET DIFFERENT PEOPLE.

SHEESH. JUST 'CAUSE SHE WON THE 'GOLDEN GLOBES' AWARD, SHE THINKS SHE'S GOT AN I.Q.

GIRL, YOU MAY FIGHT OKAY--

--BUT YOU GOT YOURSELF ONE LOUSY PERSONALITY.

WE MAY JOKE AMONGST OURSELVES, BUT NOT LIKE THAT.

PLEASE DON'T FIGHT. SOMETIMES I THINK MOST OF YOU THINK THE SAME ABOUT ME.

BUT IT'S NOT TRUE. THE ONLY THINGS I'M IGNORANT OF ARE YOUR PLANET'S CUSTOMS.

YOU KNOW, THERE ARE TIMES I REALLY PREFER MY WORLD, WHERE LOVE IS WHAT'S IMPORTANT.

-- NOT YOUR DEGREE OF EDUCATION.

19

I'M SORRY I HAD TO GET *ANGRY*, BUT YOU'RE MY *FRIENDS*--

AND WE WEREN'T *ACTING* LIKE IT. NO, YOU'RE RIGHT, HONEY--

AND I ALSO THINK YOU'RE RIGHT ABOUT *TRIDENT*--

I GOT AN IDEA. SOMEONE GET ME HIS *PIG-STICKER*.

I THINK I CAN FIND US OUR *BAD GUYS*.

SOON, IN A DILAPIDATED HIGHRISE IN NEW YORK'S WEST EIGHTIES...

HEY, C'MON-- HE WAS *HOLDING OUT* ON US.

TOLD US THAT BANK JOB ONLY GOT US *50* GRAND WHEN HE PULLED IN OVER *HUNDRED* THOU.

MAN, HE DESERVED GETTING IT STUCK TO HIM. *AITCHOO!*

BLAST IT. YOU'RE SO GOOD *INVENTING* STUFF, DO SOMETHIN' ABOUT *COLDS*, HUH?

IF I COULD, I'D GO *STRAIGHT*.

BUT ALL I'VE EVER BEEN USEFUL FOR IS INVENTING *WEAPONS* FOR THE *H.I.V.E.*

NO MORE OF THAT, EH? NOW WE'RE *FREELANCE!* AND WE'RE DOIN' JUST *FINE*.

YOU WOULDN'T WANNA *BET* ON THAT, WOULDJA, *GOOFBALL*?

WH--WHAT?

OH, MY--

AW, THEY CAN'T *FIGGER* OUT HOW WE *FOUND* 'EM.

YEAH, RUSTY TRACED YOU THROUGH THE *RADIO-WAVES* IN THAT DEAD-GUY'S *PITCHFORK*.

IT'S *OVER*, BOYS. YOU MAY AS WELL COME *PEACEFULLY*.

≈SNIFF≈ WHAT'RE YEW SO *UPSET* ABOUT, PROF? NOW WE SPLIT THE LOOT *TWO WAYS!* AITCHOOO

THE IDEA OF SLAYING TRENT STILL *REPELS* ME.

WATCH OUT, ONE OF THEM'S GOING FOR HIS *WEAPON!*

20

THAT'S WHAT I *NEEDED*.

BUDDY, IT'S *ALL OVER!*

STAY BACK. I WARN YOU. WE HAVE CAPABILITIES YOU KNOW *NOTHING* OF.

I'VE HEARD HOW *POWERFUL* YOU ARE. I CAN'T WAIT TO SEE IF IT'S *TRUE*.

BECAUSE IF IT ISN'T, YOU'RE GOING TO SEE HOW POWER-FUL *I* CAN BE.

AN *ICE BLAST?*

HARDLY EFFECTIVE AGAINST SOMEONE WHO'S *POWER* COMES FROM THE *SUN!*

NOW, COME HERE...

SKRAAK

TOO LATE, BEAUTIFUL-- *WONDY'S* GOT 'IM.

YOU'RE WRONG... WHEN I'M PREPARED, I CAN'T BE *TOUCHED*.

JUST LIKE I THOUGHT WHEN I EXAMINED THAT *TRIDENT*. YOU'RE *NOT* GOING THROUGH HIM.

SOMETHIN' ONLY *I* CAN SEE WITH MY *INFRARED* EYE.

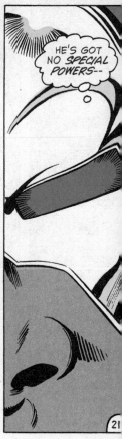

HE'S GOT NO *SPECIAL* POWERS--

21

--HE'S JUST *PROJECTING* HIS IMAGE, FROM *BEHIND* YOU!

HERA! HE SEEMS SO *REAL*...

YOU GOTTA BE CRAZY. *I* DON'T SEE ANYTHING.

WHERE *IS* HE?

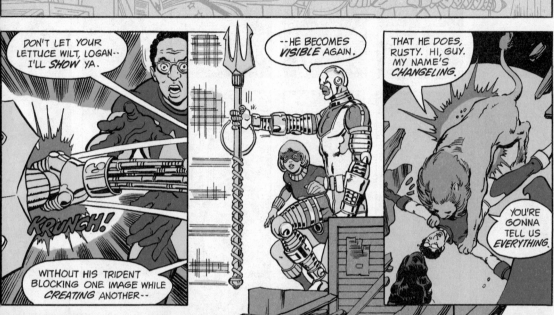

DON'T LET YOUR LETTUCE WILT, LOGAN-- I'LL *SHOW* YA.

KRUNCH!

WITHOUT HIS TRIDENT BLOCKING ONE IMAGE WHILE *CREATING* ANOTHER--

--HE BECOMES *VISIBLE* AGAIN.

THAT HE DOES, RUSTY. HI, GUY. MY NAME'S *CHANGELING.*

YOU'RE GONNA TELL US *EVERYTHING.*

AREN'T YA?

YES, YES, DON'T *EAT* ME. I WILL TALK.

HOW COULD YOU SLAY A FRIEND FOR *MONEY?*

HEY, HE *LIED...* WHAT ELSE COULD WE ... WE ... WE ...

AITCHOOO!

YOU COULD TAKE YOUR- SELF SOME *COLD PILLS,* AND GET A NICE *LONG* REST...

...FOR ABOUT TEN TO TWENTY YEARS.

PROLOGUE:

NO WORDS ARE EXCHANGED...

THEY CREEP ACROSS THE GREAT LAWN, SILENT AS BIRDS IN FLIGHT, THEN PAUSE BENEATH THE PICTURE WINDOW...

...YET EACH KNOWS WHAT THE OTHER IS THINKING.

THEY WAIT...

THEN...

NOW!

SKRASSHH!

154

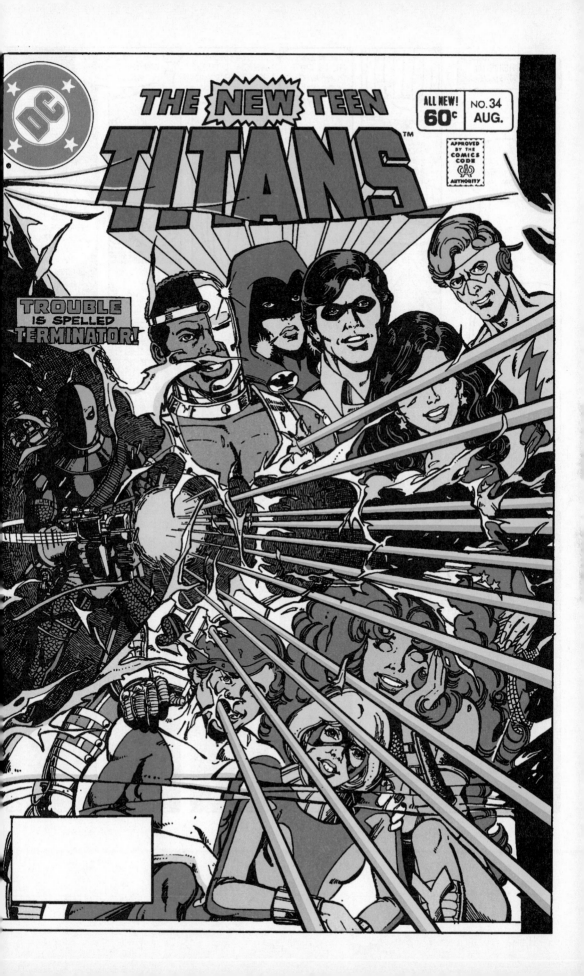

SOMEWHERE IN THE EAST SIXTIES...

I MUST SAY, SIR, YOUR NEW *DEN* BECOMES YOU.

THANKS, WINTERGREEN, I THOUGHT IT WAS QUITE AN *IMPROVEMENT* MYSELF.

MAKES ME FEEL MORE *AT HOME,* IF Y'KNOW WHAT I MEAN.

SIR, I WENT OVER YOUR *STOCKS* THIS MORNING. MOST ARE UP, ALTHOUGH THAT *VIDEO GAME* COMPANY YOU BOUGHT SHOWS SIGNS OF WEAKENING.

THEN *SELL* IT. I DON'T PLAY WITH *LOSERS.*

SPEAKING OF WHICH, I THINK IT'S TIME TO MOVE *PLAN '7'* FORWARD.

GET MY *AGENT* ON THE PHONE, WILL YOU?

WE HAVE TO WORK OUT THE *SPECIFICS.*

I TELL YOU, WINTERGREEN, BEFORE THIS YEAR IS OUT, *GOOD THINGS* ARE GONNA HAPPEN.

TO *SUCCESS,* OLD FRIEND. IT'S SO MUCH MORE PLEASURABLE THAN *FAILURE.*

BUT THEN, *THE TERMINATOR* NEVER FAILS!

AS YOU KNOW, WINTERGREEN, I HAVE SEVERAL *NEW* CONTRACTS TO BEGIN, THOUGH I HAVEN'T YET COMPLETED THE H.I.V.E. AFFAIR.

THE TEEN TITANS ARE STILL *ALIVE*, AND AS LONG AS THEY LIVE, THEY'LL BE A *BLEMISH* ON MY OTHERWISE SPOTLESS REPUTATION.

THEN YOU'LL BE NEEDING YOUR *UNIFORM*?

OF COURSE,

HIS NAME IS *SLADE WILSON*, SEEMINGLY A BUSINESSMAN UPON WHOM SUCCESS ALWAYS SEEMS TO SHINE. BUT WILSON'S STOCK-IN-TRADE IS NEITHER TANGIBLE GOODS NOR INFORMATIONAL SERVICES. FOR YOU SEE, SLADE WILSON IS A *MERCENARY*, AND HE IS THE VERY *BEST* AT WHAT HE DOES.

AH, WINTERGREEN, SOMETIMES I FEEL I MAY BE GETTING *OLD*... I KEEP THINKING OF ADELINE. THOSE WERE *GOOD* DAYS, WEREN'T THEY?

THE *BEST*, SIR. MRS. WILSON WAS AN EXCELLENT WOMAN.

NOT TO MENTION ONE HELLUVA *MARKSMAN*. OH WELL, THE *PAST* IS... PAST.

WE MUST ALL LIVE FOR THE *FUTURE*.

STILL, SOMETIMES IT IS GOOD TO *REMEMBER*.

2

ENDINGS... and BEGINNINGS!

TARA MARKOV SITS IN THE CONTROL CENTER OF *TITANS' TOWER*, HER SLIM FINGERS STRUMMING THE COMPUTER CONSOLE, A STRANGE MELANCHOLY *FROWN* CUTTING ACROSS HER YOUTHFUL FACE...

SHE HAS BEEN WITH THE TITANS FOR SEVERAL *MONTHS* NOW, THOUGH SHE WONDERS IF SHE'LL EVER BE CONSIDERED *ONE* OF THEM...

AS THEIR NEWEST MEMBER, *TERRA*, SHE POSSESSES THE AWESOME POWER TO CONTROL THE EARTH ITSELF, SO WHY HAVE THE TITANS REFUSED TO TELL HER THEIR *SECRETS?* WHY DON'T THEY TREAT HER AS A TRUE *EQUAL...?*

TERRA?

YEAH? WHATTAYA WAN--?

♪HAPPY BIRTHDAY TO YOU, HAPPY BIRTHDA HAPPY BIRTHDAY, DEAR TARA, HAPPY BIRTHDAY YOU!

GOOD EVENING, FRIENDS!

WHAT IN BLAZES--?

SWEET SIXTEENTH, HONEY.

FOR ME? I-I'VE NEVER HAD A BIRTHDAY PARTY BEFORE.

I--I DON'T KNOW WHAT TO SAY.

THAT'S A FIRST.

WE THOUGHT YOU'D LIKE IT.

I HAD MY DAD'S CHEF PREPARE THE CAKE. YOU'LL LOVE IT.

SO WHAT'S BUGGIN' YA, SQUIRT?

OH, NOTHIN'S WRONG. I WAS JUST...THINKING OF SOMETHING.

HEY, THIS IS MY PARTY, RIGHT?

OKAY. THEN STAND BACK.

FESTIVITIES CONTINUE, THEN FINALLY...

HEY, WASN'T THAT GREAT? SEE, YOU'RE ONE OF US!

YEAH? THEN HOWCUM I DON'T HAVE MY OWN CHAIR IN THE MEETIN' ROOM OR HOWCUM YOU HAVEN'T TOLD ME WHO YOU REALLY ARE?

MEBBE YOU SAY I'M A TEEN TITAN, BUT I'LL BE DARNED IF YOU SHOW IT.

4

MEANWHILE, ON THE EASTERN TIP OF LONG ISLAND...

I DON'T LIKE THIS ONE BIT. WE HAD *NO RIGHT* BREAKING IN HERE...

CERTAINLY NO *LEGAL* RIGHT, NO MATTER HOW SCUMMY SCARAPELLI AND HIS THUGS MAY BE.

WHAMP!

THUD!

YET, CHASE *IS* A DISTRICT ATTORNEY, HE MUST KNOW WHAT HE'S *ALLOWED* TO DO...

...ASSUMING HE HASN'T GONE OVER THE *EDGE*.

BLAM

YOUR GOONS ARE *USELESS*, SCARAPELLI.

NOTHING'S GOING TO KEEP YOU OUT OF PRISON-- *NOTHING!*

FOOM!

FATSTUFF, YOU'RE GOING TO *PAY* FOR YOUR CRIMES.

YOU GOT NO *RIGHT* BEING HERE.

YOU'RE TALKING ABOUT RIGHTS? MISTER, YOU'RE *SICK!*

KANK!

WHAT ABOUT THE RIGHTS OF ALL THOSE *KIDS* YOU PEDDLED YOUR DAMN *DRUGS* TO?

I-I DON'T KNOW WHAT YOU *MEAN*, CHASE. I'M AN *IMPORTER.*

I DON'T *PUSH* THAT STUFF. BUT THAT DON'T MATTER-- YOU'RE INVADIN' MY HOME. I GOT THE *RIGHT* TO BLAST YOU.

YOU'RE *SHAKING*, SCARAPELLI...YOU USUALLY HAVE YOUR *GOONS* DO YOUR DIRTY WORK?

THAT'S IT FOR *BOTH* OF YOU. THE FIGHT'S *OVER.*

HEY!?!

BAM

SPING

5

GET *OUTTA* HERE, CHASE. YOU DON'T HAVE NO *SEARCH WARRANT.*

WARRANT? YOU WANT A *WARRANT?*

AMAZING HOW YOU CREEPS WANT ALL THE *LAWS* OBEYED WHEN *YOU'RE* IN TROUBLE.

Y-YOU STILL CAN'T *ARREST* ME, CHASE. YOU'RE NO *COP.*

YOU'RE RIGHT, *I'M* NOT...

...BUT ROBIN HERE IS *LEGALLY DEPUTIZED*...THAT'S WHY I BROUGHT HIM *WITH* ME.

WHAT?

WE'LL TALK ABOUT THIS *LATER,* CHASE.

YOU'VE GOT *NOTHING* ON ME.

HERE'S YOUR WARRANT.

ROBIN, YOUR *COLLAR...*

WRONG, TUBS, THE WARRANT'S FOR ANY *ILLEGAL GUNS.* I CHECKED, YOU DON'T HAVE A *LICENSE.*

WHEN YOU *PULLED* THAT PISTOL, YOU PUT YOURSELF IN *BIG TROUBLE.*

YOU'RE *DEAD* CHASE ...*YOU'RE* A *DEAD MAN!*

I'M *QUIVERIN',* TUBS --ALL THE WAY DOWN TO MY *BOOTIES.*

WHILE, IN TITANS' TOWER...

Y'GOTTA UNDERSTAND, I DON'T *FEEL* LIKE I'M ONE OF YOU.

BUT YOU *ARE,* TERRA... WE REALLY *LIKE* YOU.

STARRY, YOU LIKE *EVERYONE.*

LOOK, Y'GOTTA REMEMBER WHAT I'VE *GONE* THROUGH THESE PAST COUPLE'A YEARS...

6

WE KNOW YOUR *PARENTS* WERE KILLED, BUT THAT'S NOT *UNIQUE* IN THIS GROUP.

MEBBE NOT, BUT HOW MANY OF *YOU* LIVED WITH TERRORISTS?

I WAS A *SLAVE* FOR ALMOST FIVE YEARS.

TERRA, WE HAVE *ALL* SURVIVED DIFFICULTIES.

THE WITCH IS *RIGHT*, KID.

YA GOTTA *ROLL* WITH THE BLOWS.

HEY, WHY DON'T WE JUST FILL HER IN ON *ALL* TITANS' STUFF?

WE *WILL*... SOON ENOUGH. AH, I'VE GOT TO *GO*.

ARE YOU MEETING *TERRY*?

I AM.

ARE YOU GOING TO *MARRY* HIM?

HONEY, I THINK I SHOULD LET *HIM* KNOW THAT FIRST.

BUT DON'T PUT AWAY THE *CHAMPAGNE*.

KID FLASH, HOW COME *YOU* DIDN'T JOIN US? TERRA DOESN'T TURN SIXTEEN *EVERY* DAY.

I DIDN'T *FEEL* LIKE IT, WONDER GIRL.

STILL HAVING PROBLEMS DECIDING WHAT TO *DO*?

NO. I THINK I'VE MADE UP MY *MIND*.

FRAN WAS RIGHT-- I DON'T *BELONG* HERE NOW. MAYBE I WILL LATER ON, BUT NOT *NOW*.

I'M GONNA *LEAVE*.

FL--WALLY, I THINK YOU'VE MADE THE *RIGHT DECISION* FOR YOU.

YOU'RE WELCOME TO COME BACK AT *ANY* TIME.

THANKS, DONNA... Y'KNOW, I ALWAYS ENJOY *TALKING* TO YOU.

YOU ALWAYS SEEM TO *KNOW* WHAT TO SAY AND DO.

7

WALL STREET, THE FINANCIAL CENTER OF THE UNITED STATES...

LITTLE DOES HE *KNOW*, EH?

WELL, THIS'LL BE AN *EASY* TEN GRAND--

AH, THERE HE IS...STROLLING ALONG LIKE HE HASN'T A *CARE* IN THE WORLD.

--NOT THAT I WOULD'VE TURNED IT DOWN EVEN IF I *HADN'T* BEEN PAID.

MAYBE THIS FITS *MY* NEEDS TOO, BUT I *NEVER* TURN DOWN CASH ON THE BARREL.

NEVER KNOW WHEN A *CHAGALL* MIGHT TURN UP ON THE MARKET.

8

CITY COMMUNITY COLLEGE...

THE OTTOMAN RULE OVER **GREECE** IN THE EIGHTEENTH CENTURY CREATED MANY CHANGES.

THE TURKS SHIFTED THE PEOPLE AROUND THEIR EMPIRE AND THAT CAUSED MANY GREEKS TO **FLEE** TURKISH RULE AND RELOCATE IN **ITALY**...

BING4!

OKAY, THAT'S IT. CHAPTERS NINE AND TEN FOR **WEDNESDAY**.

AND REMEMBER, YOUR **PAPERS** ARE DUE THE END OF THE MONTH.

PROFESSOR LONG?

OH, SALLY... WHAT **IS** IT?

WELL, PROFESSOR, I'M HAVING A REAL **HARD TIME** WITH THIS AND WELL, I WAS WONDERING--

--DO YOU DO ANY **PRIVATE** TUTORING?

Uhhh... **PRIVATE**--?

YOU KNOW--YOU AND ME. OH, AND THE **GREEKS**, OF COURSE.

I'M **SORRY**, SALLY, I REALLY AM, BUT I MAKE IT A PRACTICE **NEVER** TO--

TERRY...

D-DONNA?

OH?

HI, HONEY.

YOU'RE WEARING THE RING.

THE **RING**?

DONNA, YOU'VE MADE ME THE **HAPPIEST** GUY IN THE WORLD.

SHORTLY... SO WHEN DO YOU WANT TO *DO* IT? WE CAN GET MARRIED *NOW* OR IN THE *FALL.*

HOW ABOUT *TOMORROW?*

WE CAN FLY TO *LAS VEGAS* TONIGHT.

STOP ME IF I'M MAKING A *FOOL* OF MYSELF.

IF YOU ARE, YOU'RE THE MOST *WONDERFUL* FOOL I'VE EVER KNOWN.

IT'S JUST THAT I *DON'T* WANT TO GET MARRIED *RIGHT AWAY.*

I NEED A *LITTLE* TIME TO SEE IF I CAN *FIND* MY TRUE PARENTS.

JUST A *FEW MONTHS?* PLEASE?

DONNA, AS LONG AS YOU NEED IS OKAY WITH *ME.*

YOU SEE, TIME ISN'T *IMPORTANT* NOW. WE'VE MADE A REAL *COMMITMENT* TO EACH OTHER THAT TIME WON'T CHANGE.

MISS TROY, I LOVE YOU TODAY, AND I'LL LOVE YOU TOMORROW, AND *WHATEVER* YOU WANT I'LL GO ALONG WITH IT... HAPPILY.

MEANWHILE, BACK AT THE TOWER...

CRIPES, NONE OF YOU *UNDERSTAND* ME.

I WANT A *DECISION* *NOW.* EITHER I'M A TITAN AND GET TO KNOW EVERYTHING, OR I *WALK.*

MEBBE I'LL SET UP A STOREFRONT AND *SELL* MY POWERS TO WHOEVER *PAYS* THE MOST.

I DON'T GIVE A *HOOT* ABOUT HOW YOU DID THIS OR THAT.

C'MON, BE *SERIOUS,* TERRA. GIVE US SOME *TIME...*

10

OKAY, YOU GOT ONE WEEK.

IF YOU BOZOS DON'T THINK I'M GOOD ENOUGH TO BE A TITAN BY THEN-- *I WALK!*

MEBBE THE *JLA'LL* HIRE ME.

TARA, YOU'RE THE *FIRST* NEW MEMBER WE'VE HAD SINCE WE BEGAN...

WE DON'T HAVE ANY *RULES* ABOUT ADDING PEOPLE.

AND YOU HAVE *REFUSED* TO ANSWER CERTAIN *QUESTIONS.*

LOOK WHO'S *TALKING.* YOU ALMOST *KILLED* YOUR BOYFRIEND--

--NOT TO MENTION ATTACKING EVERYONE ELSE, LADY, IF *ANYONE'S* HIDIN' SOMETHIN'--IT'S *YOU.*

KNOCK IT OFF. Y'KNOW, UNTIL YOU CAME ALONG WE *NEVER* FOUGHT...

IS *THAT* IT? YOU *WANT* ME TO LEAVE, DON'T YOU?

IT'S *ALWAYS* THE SAME. NOBODY EVER *WANTS* ME.

LORD, I CAN'T *TAKE* IT ANY MORE. I'VE BEEN KICKED OUTTA EVERY-THING I EVER *REALLY* WANTED.

TARA...LOOK, I'M *SORRY* I SAID THAT.

LOGAN, LEMME ALONE...

...PLEASE.

SAVED BY THE PHONE BUZZER.

WHY DO I GET THE DREAD FEELING *EVERYTHING'S* FALLING APART?

I'M SURE *WALLY'S* GONNA LEAVE, RAVEN'S GOING *PSYCHO,* DICK HASN'T CALLED IN FOR *DAYS...*

TEEN TITANS HQ. BAD GUYS DON'T STAND A *CHANCE* WITH US!

OH, SARAH... HOW'M I? HEY, WHEN YOU'RE PERFECTION ITSELF, THINGS DON'T *DARE* GO WRONG, WHAT'S *UP?*

GAR, PLEASE LET ME SPEAK TO VICTOR. IT'S *IMPORTANT.*

HOLD ON. I'LL BUZZ HIM IN THE *GYM.*

VIC, IT'S **SARAH.** SHE SAYS IT'S IMPORTANT.

I DON'T WANT TO **TALK** TO HER.

C'MON, RUSTHEAD, YOU TWO WERE TIGHTER'N CHARO'S **PANTS.**

SO WHY DIDN'T SHE TELL ME SHE WAS **ENGAGED?** FORGET IT, LOGAN--

--TELL HER I'M **BUSY.** TELL HER I'M OUT SAVIN' THE **WORLD.**

MY LIFE'S LOUSY ENUFF WITHOUT HEARIN' ANY MORE **LIES.**

ER, SARAH--I CAN'T GET VIC ON THE LINE. HE'S,..UH... IN THE **LITTLE ROBOTS' ROOM.**

I'LL TELL HIM YOU **CALLED.**

YEAH, TAKE CARE OF YOUR-**SELF,** TOO.

AND, IN THE WEST-SIDE APARTMENT OF SARAH SIMMS...

WHO WERE YOU **CALLING?**

PLEASE, **MARK**--I'VE ASKED YOU TO GO.

YOU WERE CALLING THAT **BLACK** GUY, RIGHT? FORGET HIM, SARAH. WE'RE **ENGAGED.**

NO, WE'RE **NOT**-- I CALLED THAT OFF **LAST** YEAR ...LONG BEFORE I MET **VIC.**

MARK, **LET GO** OF ME ...

WE **LOVE** EACH OTHER, SARAH.

SINCE WE WERE **KIDS,** EVERYONE KNEW WE WERE GOING TO GET MARRIED.

YOU **CAN'T** CALL IT OFF.

MARK, I WON'T **PUT UP** WITH THIS ANY LONGER.

LET GO!

12

WE'RE *FINISHED*, MARK, AND IT'S BEEN *FINISHED* FOR OVER A YEAR.

DO ME A FAVOR, PLEASE -- *STAY OUT OF MY LIFE!*

SARAH, I *LOVE* YOU.

SLAM

TOUGH *COOKIE,* EH?

NO, NOT SO TOUGH.

TITANS' TOWER...

OKAY, OKAY... I WON'T *QUIT* RIGHT AWAY.

BUT YOU DON'T UNDERSTAND WHAT BEING ACCEPTED AS A TITAN *MEANS* TO ME.

AS GREAT AS I AM, BEING *ALONE* STILL SCARES ME.

I *KNOW* WHAT IT MEANS TO *ME.*

TOO MANY PEOPLE I'VE *CARED* ABOUT HAVE DIED.

JUST THEN...

TEEN TITANS' *HEADQUARTERS?* I SURE HOPE I'VE GOTTEN THROUGH.

HUH? THE *VIEW SCREEN...* IT SUDDENLY BLINKED ON.

HIM?

TERMINATOR?

UHH, WHAT'S THE *WHO*'SINATOR?

THAT'S *TERMINATOR,* GIRL-- AS IN TERMINATING YOUR LIFE. DYING. KAPUT. DAISY PUSHING TIME.

SPEAKING OF WHICH, LOGAN, I SEE *YOU'VE* RECOVERED FROM OUR LAST MEETING.

SERVES ME RIGHT FOR NOT MAKING *SURE* YOU WERE DEAD.

WHICH IS PARTIALLY THE *REASON* FOR THIS CALL.

13

Y'SEE, I TOOK OUT A **CONTRACT** WITH THE *H.I.V.E.* TO KILL YOU. SO FAR I'VE--FAILED. I *DO* HATE THAT WORD FAILED.

ANYWAY, I'M ARRANGING A **TRADE.** YOU TITANS FOR THIS PITIFUL **STOCKBROKER.** I EITHER KILL YOU OR HIM.

WHO WILL IT **BE?**

YOU FILTH, I'LL TEAR YOU--

NO.

I'VE BEEN **LOOKING** FOR A WAY TO PROVE MYSELF.

ACKK!

WHAM!

I'M GONNA TAKE ON THIS CREEP--*ALONE!*

INSTANTS LATER, A WEDGE OF EARTH SOARS SKYWARD...

...AS TERRA'S FACE TURNS **GRIM,** THINKING ABOUT THE IMPORTANT MISSION AT HAND.

WHERE'S **SHE** OFF TO? MAYBE SHE'S FOUND SOMEONE SHE HASN'T **INSULTED** TODAY.

STRANGE KID.

HELP! STOP HER! DON'T LET HER **GO!**

LOGAN?

SOMETHING'S **WRONG.**

14

WALL STREET...

ACTUALLY, MY FRIEND, CONSIDER YOURSELF *LUCKY.*

IF THIS WERE AN *ORDINARY* HIT, YOU WOULD HAVE BEEN DEAD *LONG AGO.*

BUT, YOU SEE, I *NEED* YOU. DOESN'T IT FEEL *GOOD* TO BE NEEDED?

SOUNDS FROM *OUTSIDE?* I DO BELIEVE THEY'VE *COME.*

YOU HAVEN'T GUESSED *WRONG,* MISTER.

MEET *TERRA*--THE *NEWEST* TEEN TITAN.

FWAM!

KRASH!

CREEPO, I'M GONNA PLANT YOU *SIX FEET UNDER.*

TERRA? *INTERESTING* NAME. THAT MUST BE BECAUSE YOU POSSESS *EARTH* POWERS.

THEY COULD PROVE QUITE *FORMIDABLE,* GIRL--

--*IF* I LET YOU *LIVE.*

FWAMM!

BUT THERE'S NO CHANCE OF *THAT!*

15

BUT...

THAT MOUNTAIN OF EARTH *LIFTED* YOU OUT OF THE WAY. NOT *BAD*--

GIRL, YOU'RE *BETTER* THAN I EXPECTED YOU'D BE--

--MEBBE EVEN *BETTER* THAN THOSE *OTHER* TITANS. BUT THAT WON'T *SAVE* YOU.

WANNA *BET*, ONE-EYE?

I-I *DID* IT. BLASTED THE GROUND *BELOW* 'IM...

IT SHOULD *CARRY* HIM OFF...

JUST HOPE I AIMED HIM AT THE *RIVER*... DON'T WANT HIM SPLATTERING ALL OVER THE *SIDEWALK.*

16

SHE *IS* GOOD... THIS WOULD PROBABLY *CRIPPLE* ANY ORDINARY MAN.

BUT I'M HARDLY *ORDINARY.*

MY BRAIN CAPACITY HAS BEEN INCREASED TO *90%*--I'VE GOT *FULL CONTROL* OVER MY BODY.

NOBODY *ELSE* ON EARTH COULD EXECUTE THIS MOVE SO PERFECTLY.

TERMINATOR'S SWORD FLASHES OUT, IMBEDDING ITSELF IN THE STONE WALL OF THE HANDICOTT BUILDING...

171

FOR A MOMENT DEATHSTROKE HANGS IN MID-AIR. THEN, KICKING FREE, HE BEGINS HIS FALL...

EVERY MUSCLE TENSING, DEATHSTROKE STARTS AN INNER COUNTDOWN...

TIMING IS CRUCIAL...

THEN,...

THERE SHE IS AGAIN,...NOT GIVING ME A MOMENT TO CATCH MY BREATH.

WE AREN'T DONE YET, TERMY--

--THIS TIME I FINISH YOU OFF.

DON'T BE SO SURE OF YOURSELF, GIRL.

THESE EXPLODING DISKS SHOULD GIVE QUITE A SHOW!

UH-OH ,...COMING TOO CLOSE. GOTTA MOVE BACK, OUT OF HIS RANGE ...

I HEAR HER PARTNERS CLOSING IN...

NOW IS THE TIME TO ACT.

BLAMMO!

172

THIS IS IT... C'MON, TITANS... WHERE THE HECK *ARE* YOU?

I DIDN'T GET *THAT* MUCH OF A HEAD START.

HOLD IT... FEELING A SUDDEN *UPDRAFT.* I'M SLOWLY BEING *LOWERED.*

I DON'T *SEE* HIM, BUT I BET MY LAST DONUT *KID FLASH* IS DOWN THERE.

YAHOOO! IT WORKED!

WELL, I WAS *WONDERING* IF YOU'D SHOW UP.

WE'RE *HERE,* TERMINATOR.

AND THIS TIME WE'RE PLAYING FOR *KEEPS!*

SKRREEEEE

SHE'S NOT *KIDDING.* ONLY MY SUPER-FAST REFLEXES SAVED ME FROM HER *STARBOLT.*

DON'T TAKE 'IM ALL BY *YOURSELF,* STARRY--

--LEAVE ENOUGH FER *ME* TO SMASH.

BLAM!

HOLD IT. HE'S *MINE.*

HE ALMOST *KILLED* ME. I STILL REMEMBER THE *PAIN.*

I *WANT* HIM.

BUT WHAT YOU *WANT,* CHANGELING--

18

--IS *NOT* WHAT YOU'RE GETTING.

FWAMM!

THEY'VE BECOME A *REAL TEAM* SINCE WE LAST TANGLED.

CAN'T TAKE THEM ALL ON IN AN *OPEN* CONFRONTATION.

YOU ALL *RIGHT?*

I *THINK* SO. THANKS, FLEET-FEET. YOU SAVED MY *LIFE.*

YOU WOULD'VE DONE THE SAME FOR ME.

IT'S *ALWAYS* THIS WAY--ALWAYS FIGHTING, ALWAYS WORRYING IF SOMEONE YOU CARE FOR WILL DIE OR... *CHANGE.*

I'VE *HAD* IT. I CAN'T PUT UP WITH THIS PRESSURE ANY LONGER.

SOMETHING *WRONG,* FLASH? YOU'RE *SLOWER* THAN I REMEMBERED.

HARDLY NEEDED MY *INCREASED* REFLEXES TO DOWN YOU.

OKAY, PALS AND GALS-- UNLESS YOU WANT KID FLASH HERE GRINNING OUT OF HIS *THROAT*--

--I SUGGEST YOU *BACK OFF.*

HE'LL *DO* IT.

LET ME *BLAST* HIM.

NO... CAN'T TAKE THE *CHANCE.*

YOU'RE BEING *SMART*... I'M GETTING AWAY-- EH?

THAT *S-SOUND?*

GRUMMBLE

19

174

A FIST OF EARTH? BLAST-- IT'S THAT *TERRA* GIRL.

I GOT *FLASH*...

I CAN STOP THE *OTHER* TITANS, BUT SHE KEEPS *GETTING* ME.

THEN WE CAN *MOVE IN*.

GIVE UP BEFORE I LET THAT HAND *CRUSH* YOU.

YOU'RE *GOOD*, GIRL, BETTER THAN ALL THE *OTHERS*.

BUT I STILL GOT MY *POWER STAFF*...

NOBODY CAPTURES THE TERMINATOR. *NOBODY!*

SK ABA MM!

H-HE'S *GONE?* HE BLEW HIMSELF UP?

NO TROUBLE FIGGERIN' *THIS* GAME'S *MOST VALUABLE PLAYER.*

B-BUT I *LOST* HIM... HE WAS IN MY HANDS AND HE GOT AWAY.

I-- FAILED.

NOPE. YOU SAVED MY *LIFE*, TERRA.

WELL, YOU SAVED *MINE*.

AND YOU'VE REALLY *PROVEN* YOURSELF. YOU *ARE* A TITAN.

I--I AM?

YOU *BET*, KID.

HEY, ARE YOU *OKAY?*

Y-YEAH... I GUESS I'M STILL A LITTLE *STUNNED.*

I GOTTA *DO* SOMETHING... I-I'LL SEE YOU GUYS *LATER.*

20

SHE REALLY FOUGHT HERSELF THE *GOOD* FIGHT.

I *TOLDJA* SO. IS SHE *OKAY* NOW?

I'D CERTAINLY VOTE SO.

THAT'S IT, THEN. WE TELL HER EVERYTHING-- *TOMORROW.*

BROOKLYN, NEW YORK...

TARA MARKOV HAD BROUGHT GAR LOGAN HERE TO THIS TENEMENT WHERE, SHE SAID, SHE HAD BEEN HELD *CAPTIVE* BY TERRORISTS...

NOW SHE RETURNS, A BIT *FORLORN.*

HOW HER *LIFE* HAS CHANGED...

TERRA.

HUH? *YOU?*

WHY SO SURPRISED, *TERRA?* YOU *KNEW* WE'D BE TALKING.

YEAH, JUST THOUGHT *I'D* GET HERE FIRST.

HOW DID IT *GO?*

PERFECT. THEY SWALLOWED *EVERYTHING.*

THEY DIDN'T KNOW IT'S ALL BEEN A *SET-UP.*

THEY DIDN'T SUSPECT THE *TERRORISTS* WORKED FOR YOU.

THEY DON'T SUSPECT THAT I'VE BEEN *PLANTED* IN THEIR STUPID GROUP.

21

AND THEY CERTAINLY DIDN'T SUSPECT OUR WHOLE *FIGHT* WAS WORKED OUT IN ADVANCE.

TERMINATOR, YOU PULLED OFF A CONVINCING *DEATH.*

I COULDN'T HAVE DONE IT WITHOUT THE *SAFETY TUNNEL* YOU CHANNELED.

I THINK THEY'RE GOING TO TELL ME THEIR *SECRETS* AT OUR NEXT *FULL* MEETING.

EXCELLENT. THEN THE TEEN TITANS ARE AS GOOD AS *DEAD!*

UPTOWN IN MANHATTAN...

I'M FED UP, CHASE -- YOU *USED* ME.

TO PUT SCARAPELLI BEHIND BARS I *BENT* A FEW LAWS.

MY GOD -- IF YOU HAD A *WARRANT,* WE DIDN'T NEED TO BREAK IN LIKE THAT.

I WANTED SCARAPELLI TO KNOW HE COULDN'T *ESCAPE* ME.

BUT YOU'RE A *DISTRICT ATTORNEY.* YOU'RE SUPPOSED TO *OBEY* THE LAW.

THE LAW IS *USELESS.* ONLY *JUSTICE* COUNTS.

MY GOD. AND I THOUGHT *THE BATMAN* WAS *OBSESSED.*

DON'T CALL ME *AGAIN,* CHASE.

IS IT *TRUE,* ADRIAN? DID YOU BREAK THE *LAW?*

DORIS, *SCARAPELLI* BROKE THE LAW AND HE WAS *RELEASED.*

I HAD TO FORCE HIS *HAND.*

ADRIAN, I'M *WORRIED.*

DON'T BE, HONEY. I'D NEVER DO ANYTHING *WRONG.* OR ANYTHING THAT WOULD *HURT* YOU.

22

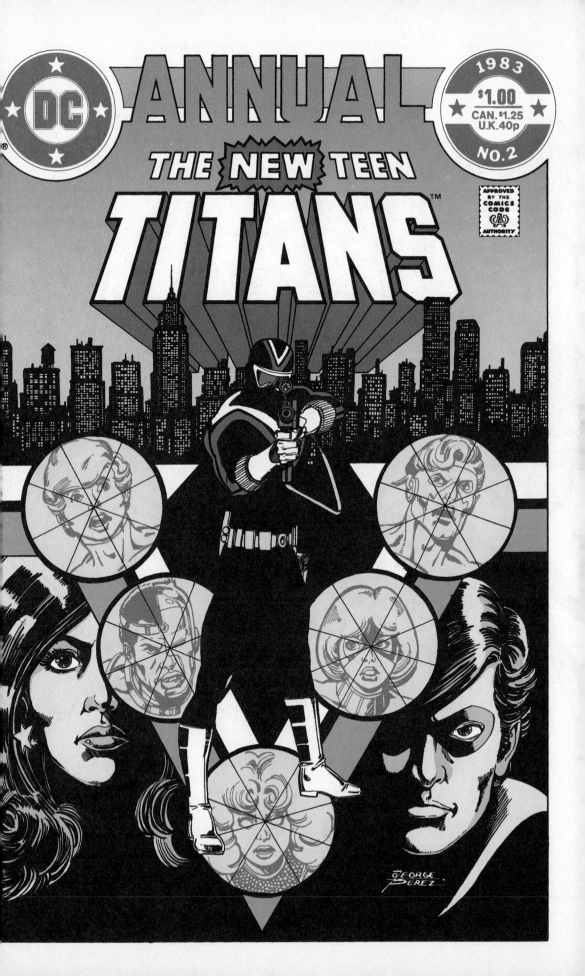

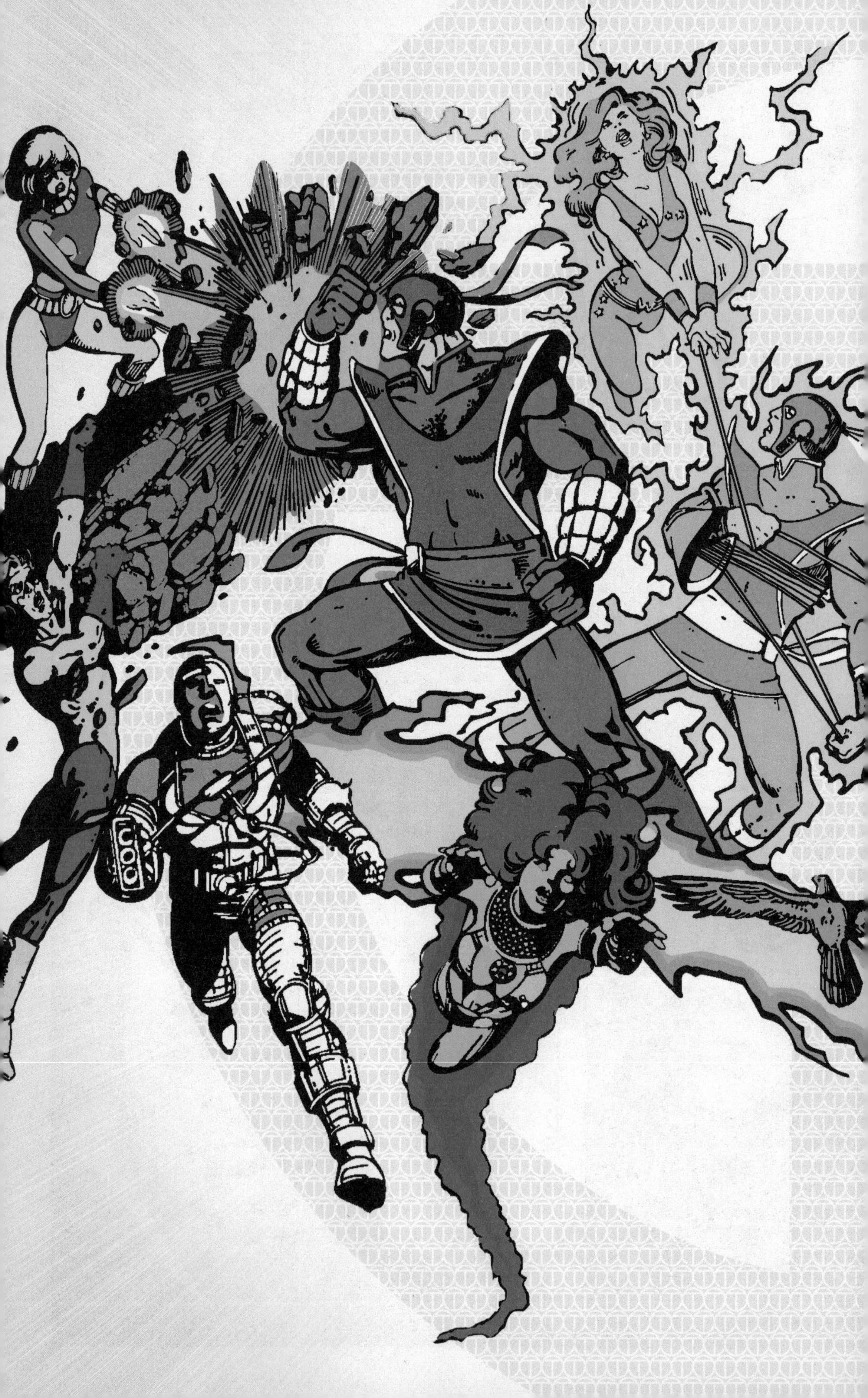

PERHAPS I CAN *SPEAK* WITH HIM.

ROBIN, WE HAVE HEARD RUMORS THAT YOU AND DISTRICT ATTORNEY CHASE BOTH PERFORMED A VIGILANTE-STYLE RAID ON THE HOME OF REPUTED MOBSTER ANTHONY SCARAPELLI. IS THAT *TRUE?*

NO COMMENT.

MR. SCARAPELLI'S LAWYER CLAIMS IT WAS BREAKING AND ENTERING...THAT YOU TWO WERE *HARRASSING* HIS CLIENT. ANY *COMMENT* ON THAT?

LISTEN. ADRIAN CHASE IS A DEDICATED MAN WHO GOT TIRED OF SEEING EVERY CREEP WITH A BUCK *BEAT* THE LEGAL SYSTEM.

MY GOD. THERE'S A MAN *DYING* IN THERE. HE MAY ALREADY BE *DEAD*--

WHATEVER CHASE *DID* HE DID TO *HELP* THE PEOPLE OF NEW YORK.

THAT'S MY COMMENT. NOW, LEAVE ME *ALONE.*

CAPTAIN HALL, DO YOU BELIEVE THAT ANTHONY SCARAPELLI MIGHT BE RESPONSIBLE FOR TONIGHT'S DISASTER?

MISS BAYE, WE HAVE JUST BEGUN OUR *INVESTIGATION.* UNTIL ALL THE *FACTS* ARE IN, THERE WILL BE NO FURTHER COMMENT.

THIS IS SANDY BAYE FOR NEWSLINE 8. WE'LL RETURN TO ROGER AFTER THIS WORD FROM "RAT-TRAP--IT SQUASHES RATS--DEAD!"

3

...LORNA TOLLE WITH THE CHANNEL 6 HOTLINE. INVESTIGATION ON THE ATTACK OF NEW YORK DISTRICT ATTORNEY ADRIAN CHASE CENTERS ON THIS MAN...

A. SCARAPELLI

...ANTHONY SCARAPELLI, A REPUTED MEMBER OF THE NEW YORK MAFIA.

ALTHOUGH MR. SCARAPELLI HAS NOT BEEN *CHARGED*, MY SOURCES IN CITY HALL SAY AN INDICTMENT IS *FORTHCOMING*.

TONY, TONY, THAT WAS NOT VERY *GOOD* WHAT YOU DID.

RUBBING OUT A DISTRICT ATTORNEY WITHOUT ADVISING THE FAMILY IS *TROUBLE*.

I DIDN'T HAVE TIME. HE WAS MOVING IN FAST. HE HAD *INFORMATION*...

CHASE KNEW *NOTHING*. IF HE DID, THAT HOTHEAD WOULD HAVE *ALREADY* HAD YOU SPLITTING ROCKS UPSTATE.

TONY, I AM SO *DISAPPOINTED* IN YOU. YOU WERE LIKE MY OWN *SON*.

IT APPEARS I MUST BECOME *INVOLVED* WITH THIS DIRTY BUSINESS.

DONNA OMICIDIO, DO YOU REMEMBER WHAT WE DISCUSSED EARLIER? HIS *RECORDS*?

I DID NOT *FORGET*, DON GEORDAN. TONY, YOU WILL BRING ALL YOUR *FILES* TO ME, TONIGHT.

GODMOTHER, I CAN'T... IT WOULD-- UH TAKE TOO LONG TO *GET* THEM ALL.

OF COURSE, TONY...I AM NOT *UNFAIR*.

YOU HAVE UNTIL *TOMORROW*.

MORNING.

4

THIS JUST IN.

CHASE

1952 - 1983

UPDATE

DORIS CHASE, WIFE OF ADRIAN CHASE, AND HER TWO CHILDREN WERE DECLARED *DEAD*...

IT'S STRANGE, CAPTAIN HALL, BUT WHEN ADRIAN SHOWED ME HIS *SEARCH WARRANT*, I REALIZED HE WAS USING ME TO *COERCE SCARAPELLI.* HE OBVIOUSLY DIDN'T HAVE ENOUGH INFOR-MATION TO GET A *CONVICTION.*

WHY DID YOU GO ALONG WITH CHASE?

I GUESS I *BELIEVED* IN CHASE ... THOUGHT HE WANTED TO *HELP.*

MY PROBLEM IS I TEND TO *FOLLOW* MORE THAN I LEAD.

WHAT ARE YOU GOING TO DO ABOUT *SCARAPELLI?*

NOTHING... *YET.* WE HAVEN'T ANY EVIDENCE *LINKING* HIM WITH THE FIREBOMBING.

OH COME ON, DON'T GIVE ME THAT *GARBAGE.*

THIS IS *LOUSY,* HALL -- DAMN *LOUSY.*

EXCUSE ME, ARE YOU ONE OF THE *TITANS?*

ENTERING THE HOSPITAL NOW ARE *THE NEW TEEN TITANS.* YES, I EVEN *RECOGNIZE* ONE OR TWO. I BELIEVE THAT'S *ROBOTMAN* COMING IN FIRST.

NO. I'M *SNOW WHITE,* AND THESE ARE MY *SEVEN DWARFS.* GET OUTTA MY *WAY.*

GAWD! THERE WERE MORE *REPORTERS* DOWN THERE THAN FLIES AROUND *LOGAN.*

WHAT HAPPENED, ROBIN? WE HEARD THE *REPORT.*

ARE ADRIAN AND DORIS *DEAD?*

HE *IGNORED* ME AGAIN... WHAT IS *WRONG,* DICK--? WHY DO YOU DO THIS TO ME?

GUYS, IT'S UP TO *US* TO GET SCARAPELLI.

I WANT HIM TO *PAY.*

5

CALM DOWN, ROBBIE--LET'S TALK ABOUT THIS BACK AT THE *TOWER.*

NO, CYBORG, I'M PURPOSELY *STAYING* ANGRY.

SOMEBODY'S GOT TO AVENGE CHASE. AND I'VE ELECTED *MYSELF.*

CUTE-KNEES, NOW YOU'RE TALKIN' *MY* LANGUAGE. HEY-- THE *DOC'S* COMIN'!

DOCTOR MATHEWS, HOW *IS* HE?

IT'S BEEN A *TOUGH GO,* CAPTAIN HALL.

C'MON, HOW IS CHASE? IS HE PULLING THROUGH?

TALK ALREADY, MATHEWS. HOW *IS* HE?

...A SPECIAL *EYEWITNESS* NEWS REPORT BROUGHT TO YOU BY "GATOR," THE BEER FOR PREPPIES OF ALL AGES...

DR. KEVIN MATHEWS OF MERCY HOSPITAL HAS TAKEN TO THE PODIUM. HE IS ABOUT TO ANNOUNCE THE *CONDITION* OF ADRIAN CHASE...

NEWS SEVEN
SPECIAL BULLETIN
7

MR. CHASE SUFFERED WHAT IS KNOWN AS *CLINICAL DEATH.* HE WAS DECLARED DEAD FOR APPROXIMATELY SEVEN MINUTES BEFORE THE FLOW OF OXYGEN TO HIS BRAIN RECOMMENCED.

X-RAYS HAVE FURTHER REVEALED A PIECE OF *SHRAPNEL* LODGED JUST BELOW HIS HEART, TOO CLOSE TO OPERATE.

THIS IS *ALLISON COOKE* FOR EYEWITNESS NEWS. WE'LL RETURN AS MORE INFORMATION IS PASSED TO US.

6

THEY CAN'T *DO* THIS TO ME. OMICIDIO GETS MY FILES, I'M A *DEAD MAN.*

AWRIGHT, IT MEANS ME AGAINST THE GOD-MOTHER. BUT OMICIDIO ISN'T GOING TO TAKE THIS *LYING DOWN.*

SHE'S A *DANGEROUS WITCH.* I'M GONNA NEED *PROTECTION.*

WE HAVE ALWAYS SERVED YOU *FAITHFULLY,* MR. SCARAPELLI.

YEAH. I KNOW, GARROTE--BUT FOR THIS I NEED SOMETHING *SPECIAL.*

I NEED--*THE MONITOR!*

ELSEWHERE...

SIR...

...THE *FILES* YOU REQUESTED...

THANK YOU, LYLA...

MR. SCARAPELLI, YOU ARE ASKING FOR...

A *DOZEN* SPECIAL GUARDS... AND I NEED THEM *FAST.*

I'M SORRY. ACCORDING TO MY COMPUTER READ-OUT, I CAN LOCATE ONLY *HALF* THAT NUMBER.

ARE YOU STILL INTERESTED IN MY *REFERRAL SERVICE?*

OF COURSE, MONITOR--GET ME AS MANY AS YOU *CAN.*

EXCELLENT. AS SOON AS THEY COMPLETE THEIR *CURRENT* ASSIGNMENTS, I'LL PUT THEM IN TOUCH WITH YOU...

...FOR MY *USUAL* COMMISSION.

7

ROGER DAILY FOR NEWS ELEVEN. THE PRELIMINARY HEARINGS FOR REPUTED MOBSTER ANTHONY SCARAPELLI BEGAN TODAY WITH THE CALLING OF BATMAN'S JUNIOR PARTNER, ROBIN, TO THE WITNESS STAND.

UNDER CROSS-EXAMINATION THE YOUTHFUL CRIME-FIGHTER APPEARED UNCERTAIN AND CONFUSED.

HE ADMITTED TO JOINING FORMER DISTRICT ATTORNEY CHASE ON A VIGILANTE-STYLE RAID ON SCARAPELLI'S HAMPTONS' ESTATE...

...AND BECAME ABUSIVE WHEN QUESTIONED ON HIS CONDONING OF VIGILANTE-STYLE JUSTICE.

MR. SCARAPELLI'S LAWYER, CARLO GIONETTI, HAS RECEIVED A COURT ORDER PREVENTING ROBIN FROM HARASSING HIS CLIENT IN THE FUTURE.

IN THE MEANTIME, ADRIAN CHASE HAS LEFT THE COUNTRY TO RECUPERATE.

THERE IS NO INFORMATION AS TO WHERE MR. CHASE HAS GONE, AND NOW A WORD FROM "TWEET"! THE BIRD-FLAVORED CAT FOOD.

11 NEWS AT ELEVEN
ROBIN
SCARAPELLI
CHASE

CAFE ITALIA, SOMETIME LATER...

BENITO, FETTUCINE ALFREDO AND YOUR FINEST *WINE*.

NO, MAKE THAT YOUR FINEST *CHAMPAGNE*. WE CELEBRATE, EH, GARROTE?

YES, SIR.

TONY, WE'LL REALLY CELEBRATE *TONIGHT*, HUH, HONEY?

GARROTE, Y'FIND OUT WHERE *CHASE* WENT?

NO, SIR. EITHER NO ONE KNOWS, OR NO ONE'S *TALKING*.

MAYBE HE DECIDED TO PUT EVERYTHING *BEHIND* HIM.

MAYBE *HE* HAS, BUT *I* HAVEN'T.

GEE. I THOUGHT HE WAS A *BOY*. BUT HE'S A *MAN*.

YOU COULD BE HELD IN *CONTEMPT* FOR THIS, PUNK.

YOU *PEOPLE* ARE IN CONTEMPT...

...OF THE *HUMAN RACE*.

I SUGGEST YOU *HONOR* IT.

YOU HAVE A COURT ORDER BARRING YOU FROM *HARASSING* MR. SCARAPELLI.

LEMME *UNDER-STAND* THIS, YOU WANT *ME* TO OBEY THE LAW?

I'D BE *GLAD* TO... RIGHT AFTER I LEAVE THIS MESSAGE. I'M *WATCHING* YOU, SCARAPELLI.

AND SOMEHOW... I'M GOING TO *GET* YOU.

I DON'T *THINK* SO, BOY. GINO!

I *GOT* 'IM, BOSS.

AN' I'M KICKIN' 'IM OUT ON HIS BUTT.

GOOD. I WAS *COUNT-ING* ON YOU MAKING THE *FIRST MOVE*. ⑨

BECAUSE I INTEND TO MAKE THE *LAST.*

SKRAKK

THAT *DOES* IT, KID.

I'LL HAVE YOU BEHIND BARS BY *DAWN.*

NO. I DON'T WANT ANY MORE *PUBLICITY.* WE'LL *FORGET* THIS, ROBIN--

--BUT *DON'T* SHOW UP NEAR ME *AGAIN.*

SCUM, I'M STICKING *CLOSER* TO YOU THAN PAINT TO A WALL.

AND I'M GOING TO HOUND YOU TILL YOU'RE WARMING THE *ELECTRIC CHAIR.*

ROBIN, PLEASE *STOP.*

WHAT ARE *YOU* DOING HERE.

MAKING SURE YOU DON'T DO SOMETHING YOU'LL LATER *REGRET.*

THIS ISN'T YOUR *BUSINESS.*

YOU'RE WRONG. I *LOVE* YOU, AND I KNOW YOU LOVE ME.

YOU'RE ALSO THE ONE WHO TOLD ME I HAD TO LEARN RESTRAINT.

NOW I THINK THE SHOE'S ON THE OTHER *FOOT.*

C'MON HOME.

SCARAPELLI, IT'S JUST *BEGINNING.*

10

WHY DID YOU BRING ME *HERE?*

SO YOU COULDN'T *LEAVE.*

DICK, PLEASE, I CARE FOR YOU TOO MUCH TO SEE YOU *DO* THIS TO YOURSELF.

I'M NOT DOING *ANYTHING.*

OH? THE DICK GRAYSON *I* FIRST MET WAS WARM, CARING... *FUN.*

THAT DOESN'T DESCRIBE YOU *NOW.*

THE *OTHERS* ALL SENSE IT, TOO. YOU'VE SHUT US ALL OUT OF YOUR LIFE.

YOU DON'T TELL US WHAT'S *WRONG.*

FOR X'HAL'S SAKE, DICK--WE ALL *CARE.* WE WANT TO *HELP* YOU.

A FEW *MONTHS* AGO YOU SHOWED YOU *LOVED* ME... I STILL WANT TO LOVE *YOU.*

STARFIRE, I...*UHH...*

DON'T TALK... PLEASE DON'T *TALK* ANY MORE.

RIGHT IN TARGET.

...BOY WONDER ATTACKS SUSPECTED MOBSTER AND CHERYL LADD TO PORTRAY MOTHER THERESA. MORE NEWS AND SPORTS AT ELEVEN...

THE SCARAPELLI MANSION...

NOK NOK

SIR, MR. SCARAPELLI TOLD ME *NOT* TO OPEN THE DOOR.

SECURITY REASONS, ANNA. *I'LL* GET IT.

MAMA MIA!

MR. SCARAPELLI!

DEAD? AS *DILLINGER!*

CHASE IS OUT OF THE COUNTRY. THAT MEANS ONLY THE *BATMAN KID*--WHAT'S-HIS-NAME-- DID THIS.

BUT, SIR, *KILLING'S* NOT HIS STYLE.

MEBBE NOW IT *IS.* I GOT TO *THINK* THINGS OUT.

I DON'T LIKE WHAT'S *GOING DOWN.*

OKAY, LOOK-- I KNOW THIS ISN'T MUCH TO *GO ON,* BUT IT'S ALL THE *INFO* I'VE GOT.

ROBIN, THIS IS PRIMARILY *CIRCUMSTANTIAL.* IT WON'T HOLD UP IN *COURT.*

CHASE AND I KNOW *SCARAPELLI* WAS BEHIND THIS. *WE* ALL KNOW HE WAS RESPONSIBLE FOR THE *"RUNAWAY"* TROUBLES.

AND FROM WHAT BATMAN'S STREET CONTACTS TELL ME, SCARAPELLI IS IN DUTCH WITH THE MOB.

SO MAYBE WE CAN *PUSH* HIM A BIT AND FORCE 'IM TO THINK WE KNOW MORE THAN WE DO.

12

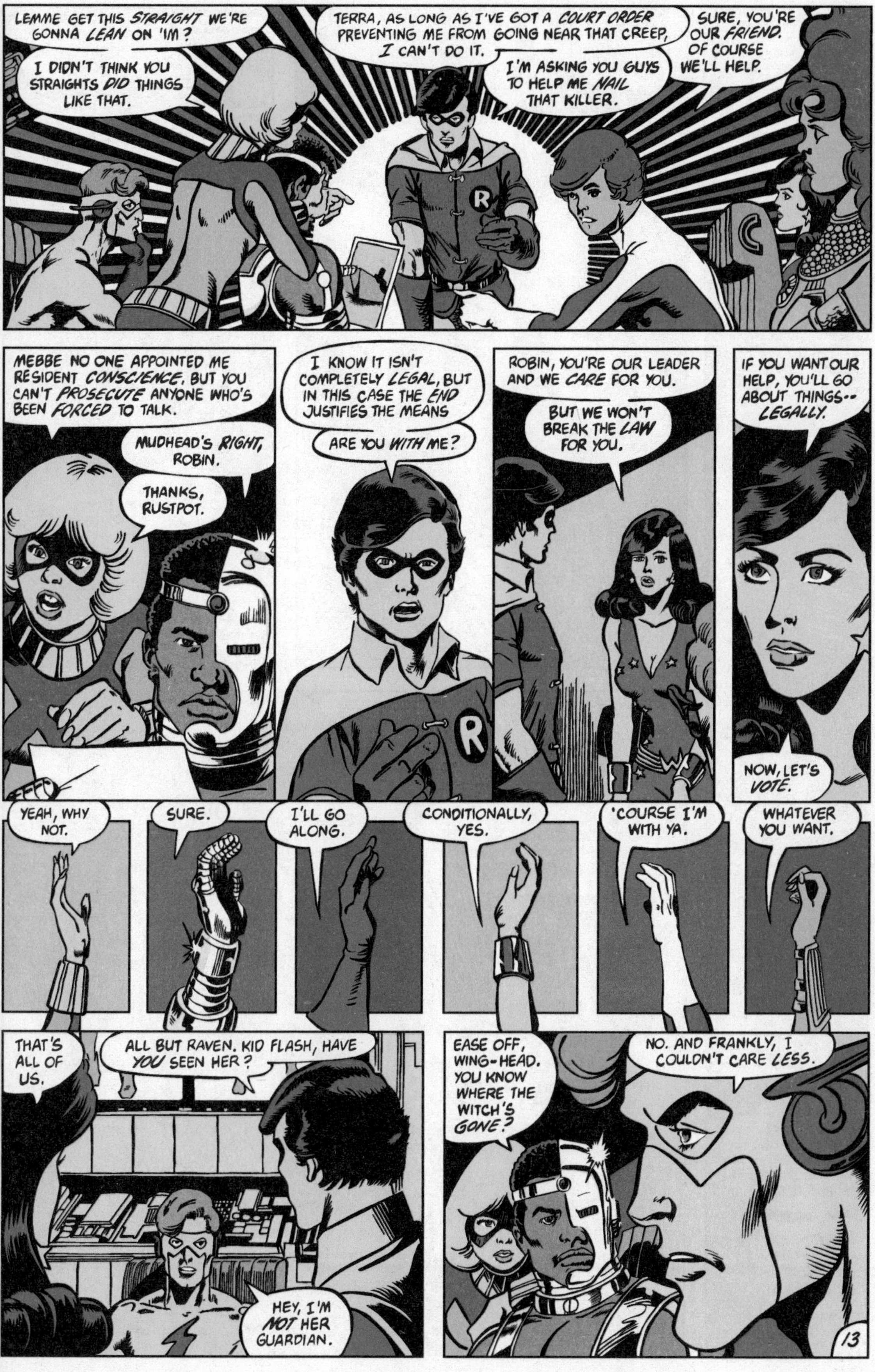

LEMME GET THIS STRAIGHT WE'RE GONNA LEAN ON 'IM?
I DIDN'T THINK YOU STRAIGHTS DID THINGS LIKE THAT.
TERRA, AS LONG AS I'VE GOT A COURT ORDER PREVENTING ME FROM GOING NEAR THAT CREEP, I CAN'T DO IT.
I'M ASKING YOU GUYS TO HELP ME NAIL THAT KILLER.
SURE, YOU'RE OUR FRIEND. OF COURSE WE'LL HELP.
MEBBE NO ONE APPOINTED ME RESIDENT CONSCIENCE, BUT YOU CAN'T PROSECUTE ANYONE WHO'S BEEN FORCED TO TALK.
MUDHEAD'S RIGHT, ROBIN.
THANKS, RUSTPOT.
I KNOW IT ISN'T COMPLETELY LEGAL, BUT IN THIS CASE THE END JUSTIFIES THE MEANS
ARE YOU WITH ME?
ROBIN, YOU'RE OUR LEADER AND WE CARE FOR YOU.
BUT WE WON'T BREAK THE LAW FOR YOU.
IF YOU WANT OUR HELP, YOU'LL GO ABOUT THINGS-- LEGALLY.
NOW, LET'S VOTE.
YEAH, WHY NOT.
SURE.
I'LL GO ALONG.
CONDITIONALLY, YES.
'COURSE I'M WITH YA.
WHATEVER YOU WANT.
THAT'S ALL OF US.
ALL BUT RAVEN. KID FLASH, HAVE YOU SEEN HER?
HEY, I'M NOT HER GUARDIAN.
EASE OFF, WING-HEAD. YOU KNOW WHERE THE WITCH'S GONE?
NO. AND FRANKLY, I COULDN'T CARE LESS.
13

ELSEWHEN...

HOW LONG HAS IT BEEN SINCE I'VE TRODDEN THE GOLDEN PATHWAYS OF *AZARATH*?

...AND YET I FEEL MORE *ALONE* HERE THAN I DO ON *EARTH*.

THE BELIEF OF AZARATH IS TRUE *PACIFISM*... NO HAND IS EVER RAISED IN *BATTLE*...

NO BLOOD IS EVER SHED BY *VIOLENCE*.

SUCH WAS THE LESSON I WAS TAUGHT SINCE *BIRTH*.

AND YET--UNLIKE ALL THE *OTHERS* HERE, I WAS ALSO TAUGHT TO *SUBDUE* MY EMOTIONS...TO *SUBMERGE* MY TRUE FEELINGS--

--TO *BURY* ANY CHANCE FOR HATRED, AND FOR *LOVE*.

FOR, IF MY EMOTIONS WERE LEFT UNGUARDED AND UNCHECKED, THE SEEDS OF VIOLENCE BURIED WITHIN ME WOULD *BLOSSOM* INTO A MOST DEADLY FRUIT.

AZARATH, YOUR WANTON DAUGHTER HAS RETURNED TO YOUR BOSOM, FOR ONLY *HERE* CAN I SMOTHER THE EVER-INCREASING LUSTS OF *TRIGON THE TERRIBLE!*

AZARATH, IF YOU WILL HAVE ME, I AM *YOURS!*

HOW MANY *MONTHS* HAVE GONE BY SINCE I'VE SMELLED THE BLISSFUL SCENT OF TRUE *PEACE*?

AZARATH, YOU ARE MY *HOME*, YOU ARE MY *ESSENCE*...

14

NO!

RAVEN, YOU *CANNOT* RETURN.

THE EVIL IS TOO STRONG IN YOU.

WE CANNOT BE *CORRUPTED* BY YOUR PRESENCE.

FOR AZAR'S SAKE, YOU MUST NOT TURN ME *AWAY*.

TRIGON'S DARK SOUL CAN ONLY BE *EXPUNGED* IN AZARATH.

WE MUST NOT LET YOUR EVIL *CONTAMINATE* US.

MONTHS AGO YOU MADE YOUR *CHOICE*.

WHEN YOU LEFT US, YOU *FORSOOK* OUR WAYS AND FORFEITED OUR PROTECTION.

WE CANNOT ALLOW YOU NEAR US *NOW*.

YOU CANNOT *DO* THIS TO ME.

YOU MUST KNOW WHAT WILL *HAPPEN*?

YOU KNOW THE *TERROR* YOU WILL UNLEASH UNLESS YOU TAKE ME BACK.

PLEASE... I BEG YOU-- HELP ME!

LEAVE US, RAVEN. LEAVE AND GO WITH AZAR'S PRAYERS.

15

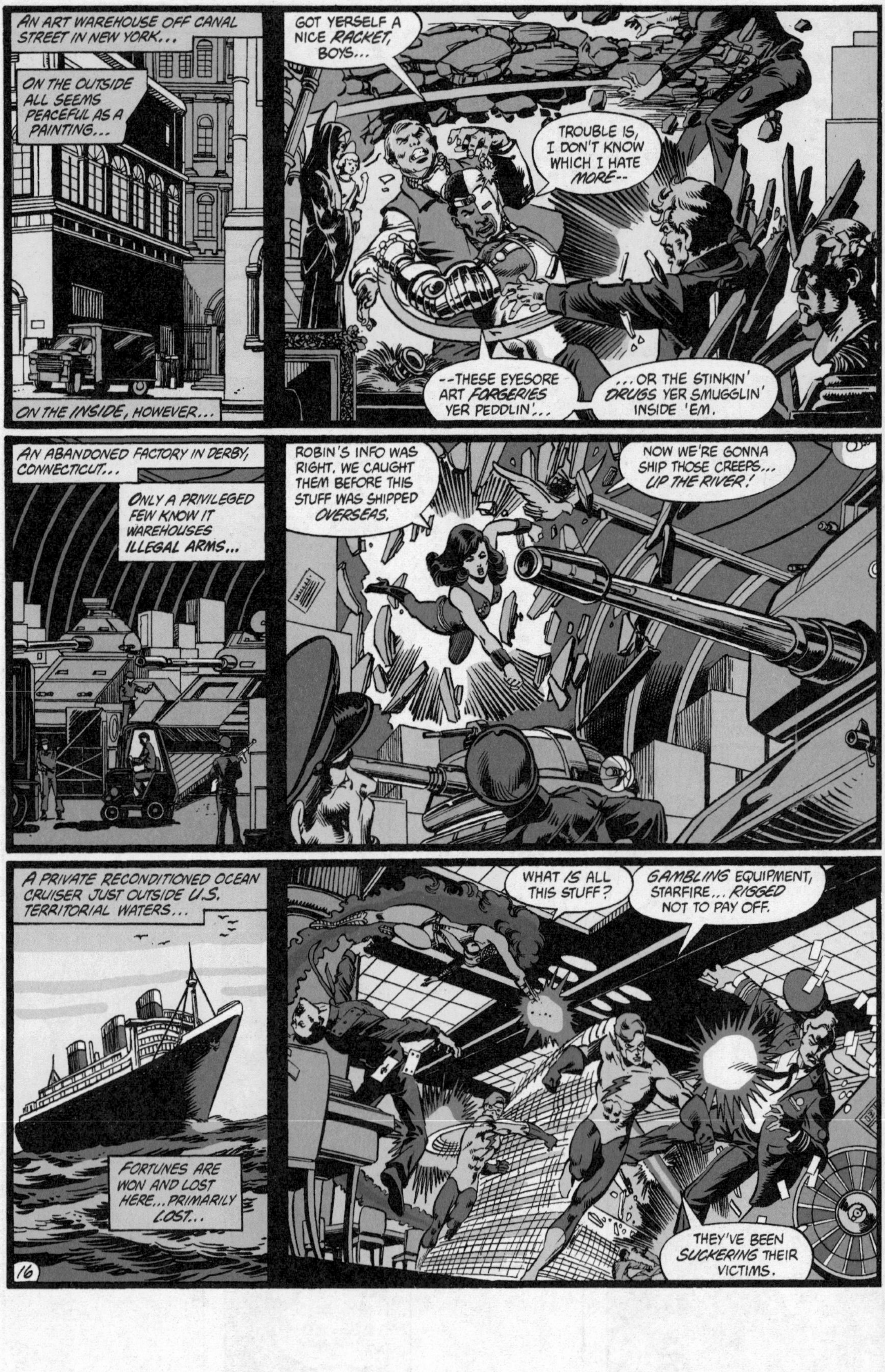

AN ART WAREHOUSE OFF CANAL STREET IN NEW YORK...
ON THE OUTSIDE ALL SEEMS PEACEFUL AS A PAINTING...
ON THE INSIDE, HOWEVER...
GOT YERSELF A NICE RACKET, BOYS...
TROUBLE IS, I DON'T KNOW WHICH I HATE MORE--
--THESE EYESORE ART FORGERIES YER PEDDLIN'...
...OR THE STINKIN' DRUGS YER SMUGGLIN' INSIDE 'EM.
AN ABANDONED FACTORY IN DERBY, CONNECTICUT...
ONLY A PRIVILEGED FEW KNOW IT WAREHOUSES ILLEGAL ARMS...
ROBIN'S INFO WAS RIGHT. WE CAUGHT THEM BEFORE THIS STUFF WAS SHIPPED OVERSEAS.
NOW WE'RE GONNA SHIP THOSE CREEPS... UP THE RIVER!
A PRIVATE RECONDITIONED OCEAN CRUISER JUST OUTSIDE U.S. TERRITORIAL WATERS...
FORTUNES ARE WON AND LOST HERE... PRIMARILY LOST...
16
WHAT IS ALL THIS STUFF?
GAMBLING EQUIPMENT, STARFIRE... RIGGED NOT TO PAY OFF.
THEY'VE BEEN SUCKERING THEIR VICTIMS.

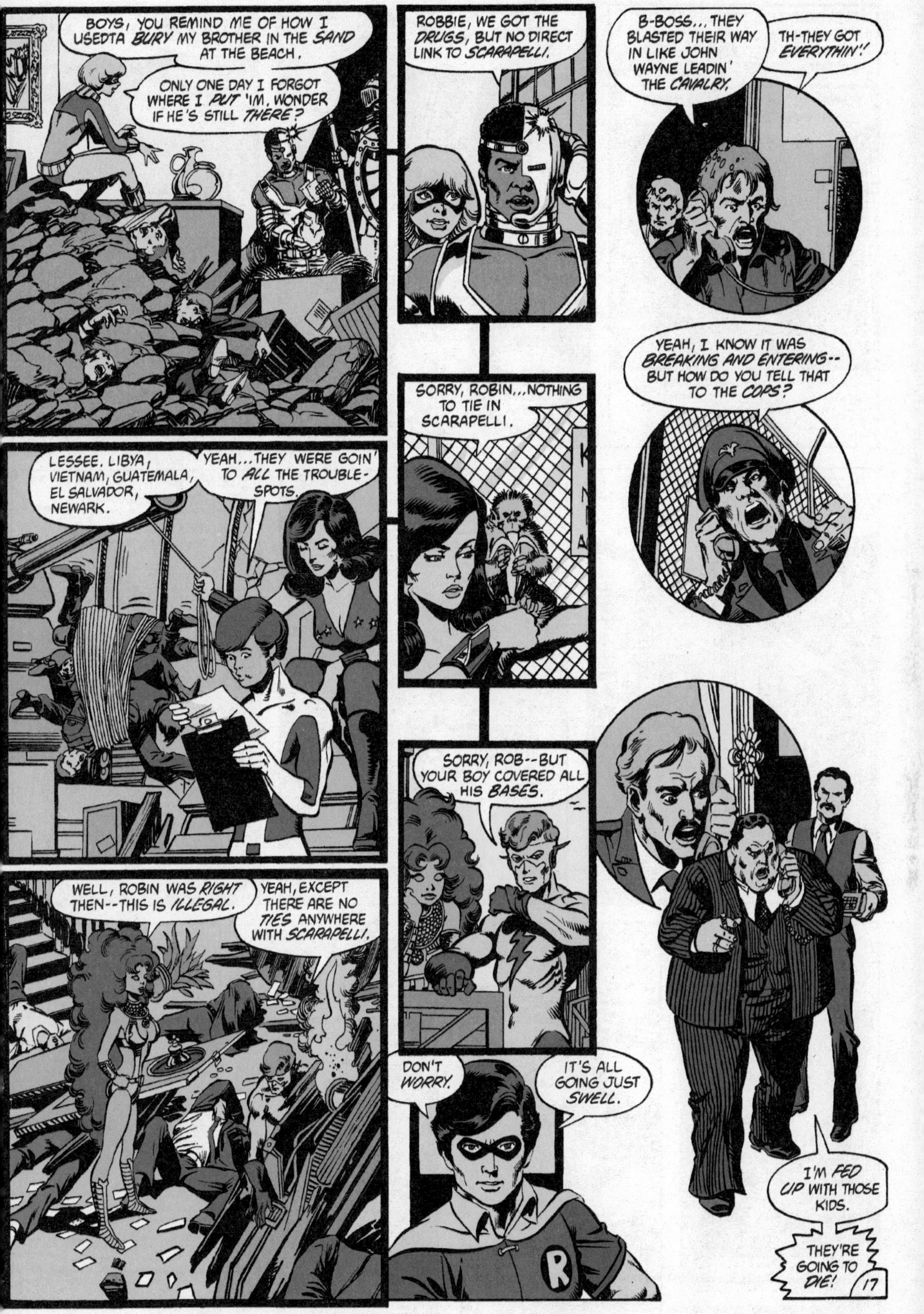

BOYS, YOU REMIND ME OF HOW I USEDTA BURY MY BROTHER IN THE SAND AT THE BEACH.
ONLY ONE DAY I FORGOT WHERE I PUT 'IM, WONDER IF HE'S STILL THERE?
ROBBIE, WE GOT THE DRUGS, BUT NO DIRECT LINK TO SCARAPELLI.
B-BOSS... THEY BLASTED THEIR WAY IN LIKE JOHN WAYNE LEADIN' THE CAVALRY.
TH-THEY GOT EVERYTHIN'!
LESSEE. LIBYA, VIETNAM, GUATEMALA, EL SALVADOR, NEWARK.
YEAH... THEY WERE GOIN' TO ALL THE TROUBLE-SPOTS.
SORRY, ROBIN... NOTHING TO TIE IN SCARAPELLI.
YEAH, I KNOW IT WAS BREAKING AND ENTERING-- BUT HOW DO YOU TELL THAT TO THE COPS?
WELL, ROBIN WAS RIGHT THEN--THIS IS ILLEGAL.
YEAH, EXCEPT THERE ARE NO TIES ANYWHERE WITH SCARAPELLI.
SORRY, ROB--BUT YOUR BOY COVERED ALL HIS BASES.
DON'T WORRY.
IT'S ALL GOING JUST SWELL.
I'M FED UP WITH THOSE KIDS.
THEY'RE GOING TO DIE!
17

STARS FRECKLE A DEEP VELVET SKY, A GLITTERING PANORAMIC CANOPY WHICH WARMS THE COLDNESS OF A VERY DARK NIGHT...

BLAST! I'VE PUNCHED THIS INFO THROUGH A DOZEN DIFFERENT WAYS--

BUT THE BEAUTY AND WARMTH OF THOSE FARAWAY SUNS DO LITTLE TO WARM THE HEART OF A CERTAIN TEEN WONDER...

--AND I STILL CAN'T FIND ANY CONNECTION.

ANTHONY SCAR

ART GALLERY OWNER : LUIGI SORRENTINO ARRESTS : 14 CONVICTIONS.

GAMBLING S OWNER ITAL ENTERPRIS INVESTIGAT IN PROGR

DICK...?

YOU NEED SOMETHING, DONNA?

YEAH. SOME STRAIGHT ANSWERS FOR A CHANGE, WITHOUT THE TYPICAL ROBIN ANGST TOSSED IN.

SO I'M IMPATIENT. WHAT OF IT?

WHY DID WE INVADE THOSE PLACES? YOU WOULDN'T LET US REPORT ANYTHING TO THE POLICE.

WE COULDN'T FIND ANY CONNECTIONS WITH SCARAPELLI.

WE'RE BADGERING HIM, AREN'T WE?

I DON'T WANT ANYTHING TO DO WITH THOSE TACTICS.

LOOK, WE KNOW SCARAPELLI'S BEHIND IT ALL. GIVE ME TIME TO PROVE IT.

WONDER GIRL WANTS TO HELP, BUT SHE KNOWS DICK GRAYSON WILL LISTEN TO NOTHING MORE.

SO, INSTEAD, SHE LEAVES...

AND WONDERS IF THERE IS ANY REAL NEED FOR THIS GROUP CALLED THE TEEN TITANS?

SHE'LL BE MARRIED SOON... MAYBE THEN IT WILL BE TIME TO LEAVE THE GROUP AND GET ON WITH HER OWN LIFE...

THE GLITTERING STARS PROVIDE WARM COMPANY AS WONDER GIRL SAILS ON THE EVENING BREEZE AND THINKS...

18

FRADKIN, YOU WERE INFORMED OF THE *PAYMENT DATES.*

YOU *REPEADEDLY IGNORED* THEM.

THAT IS WHY *I'VE* BEEN HIRED TO DEMONSTRATE TO *OTHERS* THAT IT'S NOT *WISE* TO MISS A PAYMENT.

NO--!

NOTHING *PERSONAL* IN THIS, MR. FRADKIN.

THE *SCORCHER* IS JUST DOING HIS JOB.

ISN'T THE FIRE *BEAUTIFUL?* THE FLAMES DANCING LIKE BALLERINAS. IT'S SO--SO... *ENCHANTING.*

AH WELL. SUCH BEAUTY, ALAS, IS *TRANSIENT.* I MUST NOW SEEK FURTHER EMPLOY.

SCORCHER TO MONITOR. I'VE COMPLETED THE *H.I.V.E.* CONTRACT, AND I'M LOOKING FOR MORE WORK.

I HAVE SOMETHING RIGHT UP YOUR *ALLEY.* LET ME GIVE YOU THE *ADDRESS.*

SCORCHER, YOUR LAST *PAYMENT* WAS LATE. REMEMBER, I DON'T RUN THIS *JOB REFERRAL SERVICE* FOR MY HEALTH.

19

MALAYA: THE RAINY SEASON IS OVER AND THE FORESTS ARE ONCE MORE PENETRABLE...

AT LEAST FOR SOME...

FARENTINO, YOU NO CHEAT YOUR PARTNER AGAIN, EH?

HE NO *LIKE* THAT. HE GET PLENTY *MAD.*

BUT NOW HE BE *HAPPY,* EH?

HE BE PLENTY HAPPY HE HIRE *SPEAR* TO DO HIS KILLIN' FOR HIM.

SPEAR GRUNTS WITH THE SATISFACTION OF A JOB WELL DONE BEFORE BOARDING THE *CHOPPER* WHICH WILL RETURN HIM HOME.

THERE HE WILL RECEIVE WORD OF YET *ANOTHER* JOB.

HOWARD G. CANTRELL IS BEING ESCORTED THROUGH THE MOUNTAINS WHICH SURROUND LAS VEGAS TO *TESTIFY* IN A RATHER *DELICATE* COURT TRIAL...

AFTER HIS TESTIMONY, HOWARD WILL RECEIVE A NEW NAME, JOB, AND AN UNDISCLOSED AMOUNT OF MONEY...

AT LEAST, THAT WAS THE *PLAN.*

IN REALITY, ALL HOWARD WILL RECEIVE IS A *ONE WAY KEY* TO THE NOT-SO-PEARLY GATES OF HELL...

MONITOR, THIS IS *BAZOOKA.* SCRATCH ONE CHATTERBOX.

NOW HOW 'BOUT FINDIN' ME SOMETHIN' A MITE MORE *CHALLENGIN'?*

JOSEPH, MY FRIEND, I HAVE JUST THE *JOB* FOR YOU.

20

200

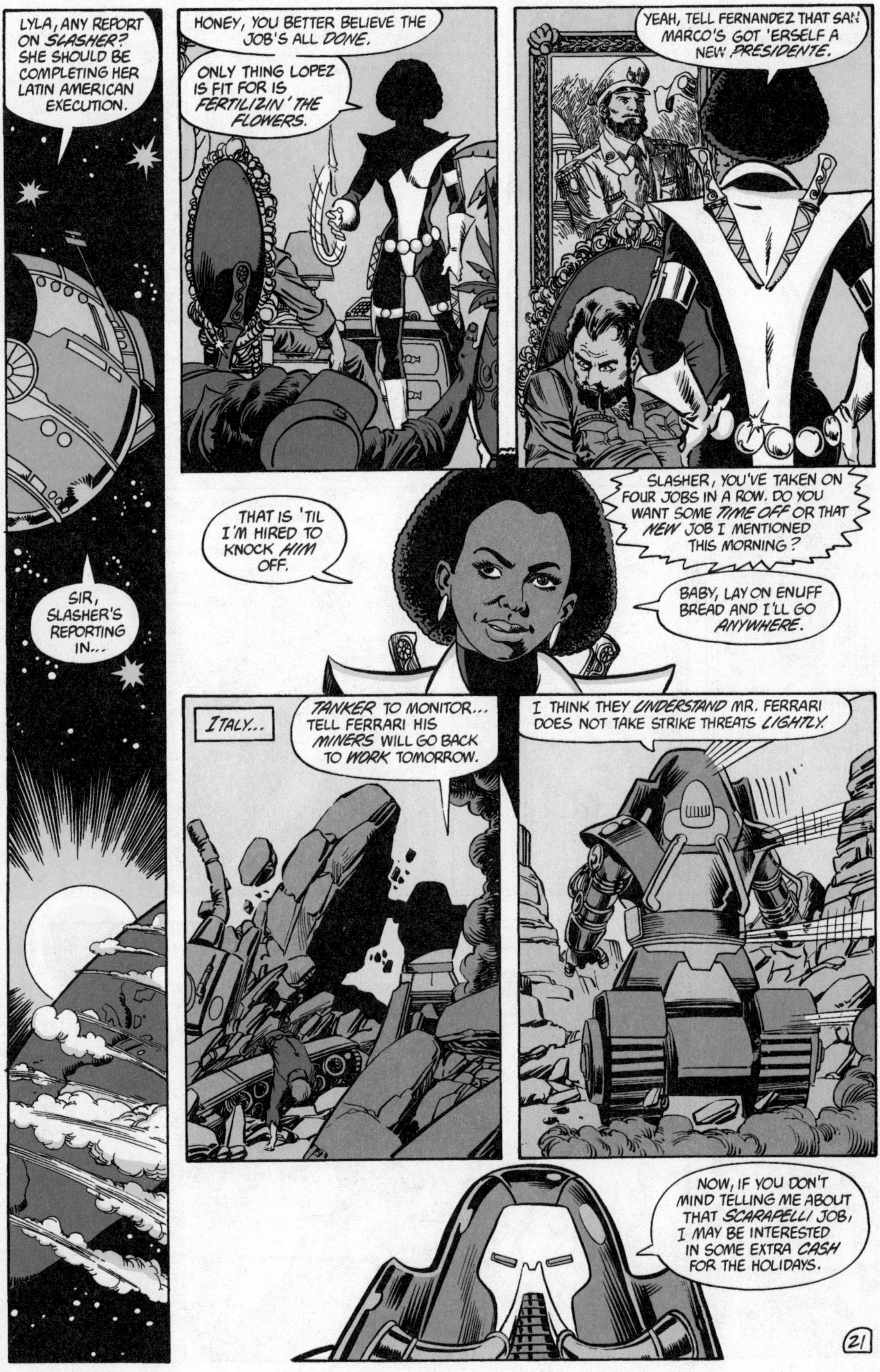

LYLA, ANY REPORT ON SLASHER? SHE SHOULD BE COMPLETING HER LATIN AMERICAN EXECUTION.
HONEY, YOU BETTER BELIEVE THE JOB'S ALL DONE.
ONLY THING LOPEZ IS FIT FOR IS FERTILIZIN' THE FLOWERS.
YEAH, TELL FERNANDEZ THAT SAN MARCO'S GOT 'ERSELF A NEW PRESIDENTE.
THAT IS 'TIL I'M HIRED TO KNOCK HIM OFF.
SIR, SLASHER'S REPORTING IN...
SLASHER, YOU'VE TAKEN ON FOUR JOBS IN A ROW. DO YOU WANT SOME TIME OFF OR THAT NEW JOB I MENTIONED THIS MORNING?
BABY, LAY ON ENUFF BREAD AND I'LL GO ANYWHERE.
ITALY...
TANKER TO MONITOR... TELL FERRARI HIS MINERS WILL GO BACK TO WORK TOMORROW.
I THINK THEY UNDERSTAND MR. FERRARI DOES NOT TAKE STRIKE THREATS LIGHTLY.
NOW, IF YOU DON'T MIND TELLING ME ABOUT THAT SCARAPELLI JOB, I MAY BE INTERESTED IN SOME EXTRA CASH FOR THE HOLIDAYS.
21

HONG KONG...

A BRITISH CROWN COLONY, AT LEAST UNTIL THE END OF THIS CENTURY...

AS TRADITIONAL AS THE *JUNKS* WHICH FLOAT UPON ITS BUSY HARBOR...

...AND AS *MODERN* AS THE GREEN PHOSPHOR-ESCENT *LETTERING* WHICH SLIDES ACROSS A COMPUTER TERMINAL...

ANCIENT AND MODERN, OLD AND NEW...THEY *COMBINE* HERE IN THIS ENIGMATIC METROPOLIS...

MADEMOISELLE *JADE,* THE MONITOR HAS AN *OFFER* FOR YOU.

SHALL I TRANSMIT YOUR *ANSWER?*

MY DEAR WEN CH'ANG, HOW MANY TIMES MUST I INSIST THAT WHEN I WORK YOU CALL ME BY MY *WORKING* NAME.

EVER SINCE I FOUND YOU AS A *CHILD,* YOU CAN ONLY BE MY *JADE.*

STILL, I WILL TRY TO *REMEMBER.*

I *HOPE* SO, WEN CH'ANG.

AS FOR THE MONITOR, TELL HIM I'VE *COMPLETED* MY WORK HERE.

AND I SHALL *ACCEPT* HIS REFERRAL. 22

GUYS, AM I HAVING *FUN* YET?

WELL, THERE AIN'T NOTHIN' *HERE*. THIS PLACE'S BEEN STRIPPED BARER THAN AN X-RATED MOVIE.

FORGET IT. I'VE SUPER-SPED THROUGH THE WHOLE *JOINT*.

EVEN CHECKED UNDER THE *COBWEBS*.

I DON'T SEE *YOU* HELPIN' ANY. BATBOY WANTS *PROOF* SCARAPELLI OWNS THIS WAREHOUSE.

THERE'S ABSOLUTELY *ZILCH* HERE.

BUT I DON'T SEE ANY *FILES*.

FRANKLY, I THINK THIS IS *ROBIN'S* FIGHT. NOT *OURS*.

ROBIN WAS SO *CERTAIN* WE'D FIND--

HOLD IT. KEEP QUIET. INTERNAL AMPLIFIER'S PICKIN' UP *SOUND*. LEMME GET A *BEAD* ON IT.

BESIDES *COCKROACHES* WITH BAD *TASTE?*

WHO'D BE *HERE?*

HE'S *DEPENDING* ON US. WE CAN'T LET HIM DOWN.

Y'WANNA *BET* 'BOUT THAT?

AND NOT EVEN THEY WOU - *AARRRGGHHH!*

GAR?!

MY GOD. WHAT *HAPPENED?*

ADRIAN CHASE'S FAMILY *DIED*. I WANT THOSE KILLERS, TOO.

STILL, ROBIN ASKED US TO *CHECK* IT OUT.

THUNK

(23)

JUST THEN...

WE'VE BEEN *HIT*. THEY'RE ALL *AROUND* US.

AGHHH! MY LEG.!!

F-FIRE'S EVERYWHERE... C-CAN'T *THINK* STRAIGHT...

C-CAN'T USE MY POWERS. I--I NEED *HELP!!*

X'HAL! TERRA'S *TRAPPED* IN THERE... AND I CAN'T DO *ANYTHING.*

OH, NO-- SHE'S *FALLING.* PLEASE DON'T BE *HURT--*

HOLD ON, TERRA-- SOMEHOW I'LL GET *THROUGH...*

'EY, BLACKY, GOOD *SPEARCHUCKIN';* BOY, YEW *SHORE* GOT THAT GREEN ONE RIGHT THROUGH THE *TAIL!*

MY NAME IS *SPEAR.*

CALL ME THAT OR *NOTHIN';* EH?

NO *FIGHTING,* FRIENDS--WE'RE ALL BEING PAID TO SEE THE *SAME JOB* DONE.

STILL, DID YOU SEE HOW QUICKLY MY BEAUTIFUL FLAMES CUT *THROUGH* THEM?

MY FIRE *INSPIRES* US TO GREATNESS.

UNHHH... THE FIRE MUST'VE *THROWN* ME... I DIDN'T SEE THAT *SPEAR* COMIN' UNTIL IT WAS ALMOST *TOO LATE...*

CAN'T EVEN *MOVE* AS FAST AS I SHOULD...

BUT I'VE BEEN RUNNING SLOWER FOR *DAYS* NOW-- AS IF I'M LOSING MY SUPER-SPEED...

24

FIRE'S EVERYWHERE... *BURNIN' UP.* C-CAN'T LET IT *KILL* ME...

STILL HAVEN'T LEARNED THE TITANS' *IDENTITIES...* TERMINATOR *NEEDS* 'EM.

GOTTA *FORCE* MYSELF TO USE MY POWERS--

--PUSH UP THE *EARTH* ALL AROUND ME...USE IT TO *SMOTHER* THE FLAMES...

AHHH...IT'S SO *COOL...* FEELS SO *GOOD...*

GOOD, GOT ME THE COLORED KID *FIRST...* BLEW HIS MISERABLE LITTLE *LEG* RIGHT OFF.

I'LL LET 'IM *SUFFER* A MITE MORE BEFORE BLOWIN' 'IM TO GOOD LITTLE COLORED BOY *HEAVEN.*

DON'T *BELIEVE* IT, GARBAGE-MOUTH!

THE DAYS ARE OVER WHERE PEOPLE HAVE TO SUFFER FOR THE LIKES OF *YOU.*

MISTER, YOU BELONG BURIED IN THE PAST WITH YOUR IDIOTIC BIGOTRIES--

WONDER GIRL, I'M AFRAID. I CAN'T LET YOU *HURT* BAZOOKA.

AS MUCH AS I FIND HIS BIGOTRY *REPULSIVE,* FOR THE TIME BEING WE'VE CONTRACTED FOR THE *SAME* WORK.

AND OUR JOB IS TO *KILL YOU!*

WHAT?

HIS FISTS ARE *SOLID STEEL...* THEY'RE LIKE *BATTERING RAMS!*

ARRHHH!! F-FEEL LIKE HE'S BROKEN MY *BONES...* MY HIP...AND SIDE ARE *KILLING* ME.

25

I COULD FIGHT ALONG WITH THE OTHERS, BUT I THINK I'D BE MORE USEFUL SNUFFING OUT THE *FIRE*.

COME TO THINK OF IT, IT'S *DICK* WHO MAKES ME FEEL THIS WAY--

USEFUL! UNTIL RECENTLY I NEVER FELT AS *USELESS* AS I DO THESE DAYS.

HE PURPOSELY *IGNORES* ME... BUT IN MY HEART I DON'T BELIEVE IT'S BECAUSE HE DOESN'T *LOVE* ME.

DONNA SAID IT BEST--HE'S TRYING TO BE LIKE *THE BATMAN*--COLD, CALCULATING... EMOTIONLESS.

TO ADMIT HE *LOVES* ME WOULD MEAN HE'S *FAILED* AT HIS GOAL--

AHH, I THOUGHT I SAW A *WATER TOWER* UP HERE... JUST WHAT I NEED TO *DOUSE* THE--

THAT WOULD HAVE BEEN QUITE A *GOOD PLAN,* STARFIRE--

--AND TO THINK, I HAD HEARD YOU WERE THE *STUPID* ONE.

UNGHHH!

SLAMM

A WOMAN UP THERE?

BUT HOW DID SHE SNEAK BEHIND ME WITHOUT MY *HEARING* HER?

KRASH

AH, DEAR STARFIRE, YOU MAY BE *SMARTER* THAN I BELIEVED, BUT YOU ARE AS *BEAUTIFUL* AS I WAS TOLD.

IT'S A *SHAME* THEN THAT I MUST *SCAR* SUCH LOVELY FEATURES, EH?

WHO ARE YOU?

I'D LOVE TO TELL YOU MY *REAL* NAME, BUT I *NEVER* MIX BUSINESS WITH PLEASURE...

BUT PLEASE... FOR THE *LIMITED* TIME YOU HAVE REMAINING--

--CALL ME *CHESHIRE!*

26

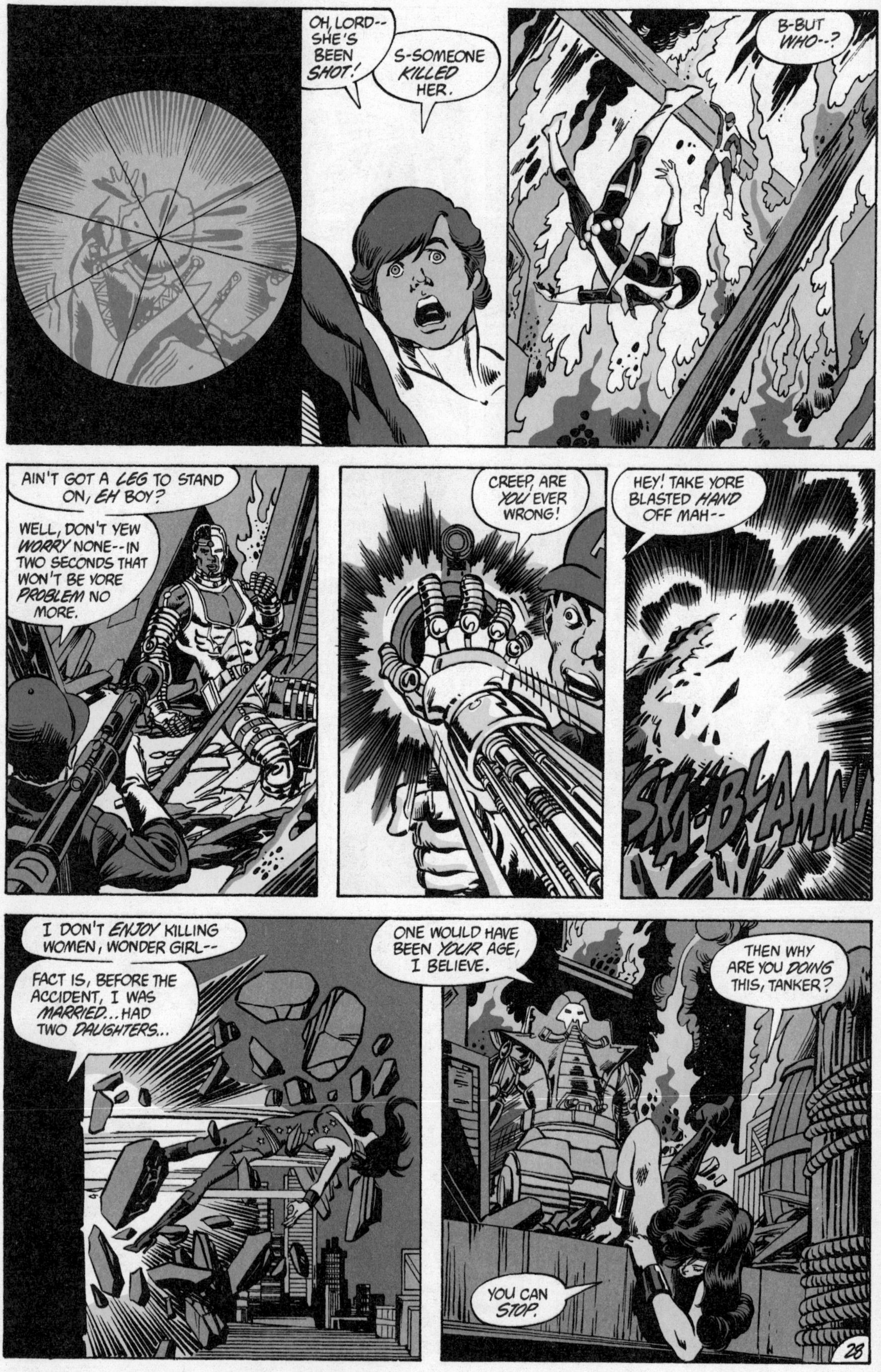
OH, LORD-- SHE'S BEEN SHOT!
S-SOMEONE KILLED HER.
B-BUT WHO--?
AIN'T GOT A LEG TO STAND ON, EH BOY?
WELL, DON'T YEW WORRY NONE--IN TWO SECONDS THAT WON'T BE YORE PROBLEM NO MORE.
CREEP, ARE YOU EVER WRONG!
HEY! TAKE YORE BLASTED HAND OFF MAH--
SKA-BLAMMM
I DON'T ENJOY KILLING WOMEN, WONDER GIRL--
FACT IS, BEFORE THE ACCIDENT, I WAS MARRIED...HAD TWO DAUGHTERS...
ONE WOULD HAVE BEEN YOUR AGE, I BELIEVE.
THEN WHY ARE YOU DOING THIS, TANKER?
YOU CAN STOP.
28

I SUPPOSE I COULD, IF I *WANTED* TO.

BUT EVER SINCE THE ACCIDENT, I'VE COME TO *ENJOY* MY NEW LIFE AS A MERCENARY.

THERE'S A SATISFYING FEELING OF *POWER* IN KNOWING THAT I CAN KILL *ANYONE* I CHOOSE AND NEVER BE *STOPPED.*

IT MAKES UP FOR SO MUCH OF MY *LOSS.*

HE'S *INSANE,* YET HE'S STRONG ENOUGH TO *CARRY OUT* HIS THREAT.

HE'LL *STRANGLE* ME UNLESS I CAN SUMMON ALL MY INNER STRENGTH.

HELP ME, HERA--

-- HELP ME STOP THIS MADMAN!

BA-WHOOM

WHEW, IT'S *OVER...* FUNNY, AWHILE AGO I THOUGHT ABOUT *QUITTING.*

BUT MAYBE PREVENTING LUNATICS LIKE HIM FROM INFLICTING HIS INSANITY ON THE REST OF US IS THE *REASON* I STICK THIS OUT.

SOMEONE'S GOT TO DO THE JOB.

YO! WONDY--NOT *SHABBY.*

YOU FIGURE OUT WHAT THIS IS ALL *ABOUT?*

NO IDEA, CYBORG, THEY WERE OBVIOUSLY *HIRED* TO KILL US--BUT I DON'T KNOW *WHY,* OR BY *WHOM.*

MEBBE WE OUGHTA MAKE ONE OF 'EM *TALK.*

HEY, RED-- Y'THINK YOU CAN GET *"MR.T"* THERE TO *CHIRP?*

KID, WHEN WE'RE THROUGH, HE'LL BE SINGING *ARIAS.*

WHOM

RIGHT, HANDSOME?

29

YEAH, KID-- C'MON RIGHT AHEAD A BIT.

YOU'RE ALMOST IN RANGE.

I ENVY YOU, KID-- YOU'LL FEEL WHAT MY LOVELY FLAMES CAN DO WHEN THEY CARESS YOU.

SCORCHER, PUT DOWN YOUR FLAME-THROWER.

HUH? MISTER, I DON'T KNOW WHO YOU ARE--

--BUT YOU'RE GONNA FRY!

I GAVE YOU A CHANCE, SCORCHER.

THAT'S MORE THAN YOU'VE EVER DONE FOR YOUR VICTIMS.

I DON'T BELIEVE THIS-- I'VE FOUGHT AGAINST WARRIORS FROM TWO DOZEN WORLDS--

--ON OKAARA I NEVER MISSED--

--BUT I CAN'T EVEN GET CLOSE TO CHESHIRE.

HONEY, YOU'RE AIMING FAR TOO WIDE TO BE EFFECTIVE.

STILL, YOU'RE A GOOD FIGHTER, I CAN TELL THAT.

YOU REALLY DESERVE A BETTER FATE THAN YOU'LL BE GETTING.

STAND STILL, BLAST YOU!

SORRY, HONEY-- NO CAN DO--

30

SHE DOESN'T *HAVE TO*, CHESHIRE--

YOU SEE, WE TITANS *STICK TOGETHER*.

AND NO MATTER HOW *FAST* YOU ARE AGAINST STARFIRE--

--YOUR *SPEED* MEANS *NOTHING* TO ME.

WELL, *HONEY*, I DON'T NEED TO MOVE FAST FOR A *HUNK* LIKE YOU.

MY *POISONOUS* CLAWS.

TASTE MY *CLAWS*, SWEETS.

IN SECONDS YOU'LL BE *PARALYZED*. AND IN MINUTES, WHY YOU'LL BE--*DEAD!*

IT'S BEEN A REAL *PLEASURE*, HONEY.

WHAT A *SHAME* IT HAS TO *END* SO SOON.

I REALLY COULD HAVE *GOTTEN OFF* WITH A GUY LIKE YOU.

BLAM

X'HAL-- *WALLY!* H-HE'S SO *HOT*...HE'S BURNING UP.

SOMEBODY-- *DO SOMETHING* BEFORE HE DIES!

RAVEN?!?

C-COLD...SO C-COLD... R-RAVEN...R-RAVEN... FOR GOD'S SAKE... WHERE *ARE* YOU?

31

HOW DID YOU KNOW?

I AM HERE.

KETTLE-BRAIN'S RIGHT-- SHE *IS* A WITCH!

I *SENSED* HIS PAIN... I WAS AWARE OF HIS NEEDS.

IF HE IS NOT ALREADY DOOMED, MY POWERS MIGHT BE ALL THAT CAN SAVE HIM.

RAVEN, IF *TRIGON* FREES HIMSELF BECAUSE YOU--

WONDER GIRL, I--I *MUST* DO THIS.

...THIS JUST IN. A FIRE HAS BROKEN OUT AT THE SCORPIO MERCHANDISING DOCKSIDE WAREHOUSE. FOR AN ON-THE-SCENE REPORT, LET'S SWITCH TO CAL DAVIS...

FIRE

THOUGH POLICE WILL NOT CONFIRM IT, REPORTS ARE CIRCULATING THAT THE TEEN TITANS WERE SEEN ENTERING THE WAREHOUSE MOMENTS BEFORE THE FIRE BEGAN...

J..JUST SPOKE WITH LOGAN. THE DOC'S TOLD HIM TO *REST.* HE SENDS HIS *LOVE*...'SPECIALLY TO GOLDIE.

ROBIN, I CAN'T GO ALONG WITH THIS ANY LONGER.

WE'VE ALWAYS WORKED *WITH* THE LAW, BUT NOW YOU'RE TURNING US INTO *VIGILANTES.*

GIVE US ONE PIECE OF FACTUAL EVIDENCE AND WE'LL BE RIGHT ALONGSIDE YOU.

YOU SHOULD BE ANYWAY. ROBIN'S NEVER LED US WRONG.

HE'S NEVER BEEN THIS EMOTIONALLY *INVOLVED* BEFORE, EITHER.

32

212

IF YOU'RE DONE CHASTISING ME, LISTEN TO THIS.

WELL, DON'T STAND THERE GAWKING...YOU DON'T HAVE TO STARE AT A TAPE RECORDER.

THAT'S ADRIAN CHASE'S VOICE.

ROBIN, I'M ACTUALLY GETTING HARD EVIDENCE, BUT FRANKLY, BOY, I'M WORRIED.

SCARAPELLI KNOWS I'VE OVERHEARD ONE OF HIS SECRET MEETINGS...

I THINK HE'S GOING TO TRY TO KILL ME. JUST HAVE TO HOPE HE FAILS.

HE MADE THIS BEFORE THE BOMBING? BLAST. WHY DIDN'T HE ASK FOR HELP?

THAT ISN'T CHASE'S STYLE. KEEP LISTENING.

THE MOB WANTS HIM OUT, BUT BEFORE THEY KILL HIM, THEY NEED CERTAIN INCRIMINATING RECORDS HE'S KEPT.

BUT SCARAPELLI KNOWS HE'S GOING TO BE SHARK BAIT, SO HE'S PLANNING A LITTLE SURPRISE FOR HIS PALS-- --ON WEDNESDAY, AT HIS DESERT PROPERTY.

ROBBIE, I ALSO HEAR HE'S HIRED SOME SPECIAL HITMEN TO GET YOU GUYS. SO WATCH OUT.

BUT, IF SOMETHING HAPPENS TO ME, GET OUT THERE AND STOP HIM.

TAKE CARE, KIDDIE COPS. HOPE TO SEE YOU AGAIN.

WELL?

WHAT CAN I SAY?

LET'S GO!

WEDNESDAY AT DAWN...

A COLD, HOWLING WIND RAISES EXPECTATIONS OF...

...DEATH.

I SEE HIS LIMO.

DO YOU THINK HE'LL BRING THOSE FILES?

MAYBE, MAYBE NOT, BUT THEY'RE NOT IMPORTANT TO ME NOW.

ANTHONY HAS BROUGHT EMBARRASSMENT TO THE FAMILY.

HE HAS ALSO DISOBEYED US.

PUNISHMENT IS IN ORDER.

33

WHAT DO YOU MEAN? EXPLAIN YOURSELF, GIRL.

I DON'T *LIKE* HER. KILL HER!

JOSEPH, JOSEPH...DON'T BE SO *RASH.*

YOU MUST *LISTEN.* ANTHONY SCARAPELLI INTENDS TO *DESTROY* YOU ALL.

THAT DAMN GIRL, SHE'LL BLOW EVERYTHING.

THE *MONITOR* SAID THE MEN WOULD BE IN *PLACE.*

GOOD. Y'KNOW SOMETHIN'--?

"*OMICIDIO LAUGHED* AT ME BACK IN THE SIXTIES FOR INSTALLIN' A *BOMB* SHELTER ON THIS LAND.

"NOW I'M HAVING THE *LAST LAUGH!*"

THERE!

35

THE LAST LAUGH... HOW FOOLISH THAT THOUGHT...

AN ACKNOWLEDGEMENT OF ULTIMATE HOPELESSNESS.

FOR THE FINAL LAUGH IS MERELY A HOLLOW, MOCKING CRY OF DESPAIR...

TWO SIDES AT ODDS WITH EACH OTHER, EACH SEEKING A VICTORY THAT CANNOT BE CLAIMED.

AND INTO THIS VALLEY OF DEATH WALKS RAVEN.

AND EACH DEATH...

...REMOVES THAT MUCH MORE OF HER SOUL.

WHAT LITTLE IS LEFT.

THEN...

I HAVEN'T FORGOTTEN.

THIS TIME SCARAPELLI AIN'T GETTIN' AWAY.

REMEMBER, WE'RE HERE TO STOP THE FIGHTING, NOT ADD TO IT.

AS MUCH AS I WISH I COULD.

36

C'MON, MOVE IT. I DON'T WANT TO BE ANYWHERE *NEAR* HERE.

SIR, IF I MAY ASK, WHY DID YOU SHOW UP IN THE FIRST PLACE?

YOU *COULD* HAVE REMAINED HOME.

YOU CRAZY? I HADDA MAKE SURE THE *GODMOTHER* WAS THERE.

ALSO, I DIDN'T EXPECT THOSE *BRATS* TO SHOW.

IT SHOULD'VE BEEN *CLEAN.* NO PROBLEMS.

SUDDENLY REALIZED... WHERE'S DICK?

HE'S NOT HERE.

DON'T LIKE DOIN' THIS...STOMPIN' OUT THE *MOB.*

BUT I GOTTA KEEP *PRETENDIN'* TO BE A *TITAN*--

--TILL ALL THEIR INFO IS *MINE!*

THEY'RE FALLIN', BUT I KEEP WONDERIN'--

--WHERE'D A HOOD LIKE SCARAPELLI GET SOUPED-UP ASSASSINS LIKE THESE?

DICK SHOULD BE HAPPY... HE'S GOTTEN THE *PROOF* HE WANTS.

NOW MAYBE HE CAN *SETTLE DOWN...* MAYBE WE CAN GET BACK TOGETHER AGAIN.

CAN YOU CALL OFF THIS WASTEFUL KILLING? NO ONE CAN WIN.

I'LL CALL IT OFF, LADY--

--WHEN ANTHONY SCARAPELLI IS *DEAD!*

37

THE EASTERN TIP OF LONG ISLAND. ONLY THE VERY *RICH* CAN AFFORD TO LIVE HERE...

BUT, AS ANTHONY SCARAPELLI WILL MOMENTARILY LEARN, NOT EVEN WEALTH CAN BUY YOU...LIFE.

C'MON, I GOT A PRIVATE JET THAT'LL TAKE US TO *HAITI.*

AND WITH THESE RECORDS, DONNA OMICIDIO WON'T DARE TOUCH ME.

THEY COULD BLOW THE *LID* OFF THE WHOLE BLASTED MOB.

THAT IS WHAT I'VE BEEN *WAITING* FOR.

WHAT?

WH-WHO ARE YOU?

YOU ARE *GUILTY* OF CRIMES AGAINST YOUR FELLOW MAN.

YOU HAVE PROVEN A LACK OF CONCERN FOR ANY OTHER THAN YOURSELF.

IF YOU WERE *POOR*, IF YOU WERE AN ORDINARY MAN, YOU WOULD HAVE BEEN *IMPRISONED* YEARS AGO...

BUT YOUR WEALTH AND YOUR POLITICAL CONNECTIONS HAVE BOUGHT YOU YOUR FREEDOM TIME AND TIME AGAIN.

YOUR WEALTH CANNOT BUY *ME.*

AND YOUR POLITICAL CONNECTIONS WON'T FREE YOU WHEN THE CONTENTS OF THESE BOOKS ARE REVEALED.

YOU'RE FINISHED.

WHO ARE YOU?

38

DON'T TRY TO RUN, SCARAPELLI.

YOU WON'T ESCAPE ME.

WHO IN HELL'S NAME ARE YOU?

I'M ALL THE *LAWS* YOU'VE FLOUTED.

I'M ALL THE *VICTIMS* YOU'VE MADE SUFFER.

I'M ALL THE *DREAMS* YOU'VE CRUSHED.

FOR GOD'S SAKE, MAN-- WHO ARE YOU?

I'M *JUSTICE* NO LONGER BLIND.

OH, GOD-- YOU!

39

219

CHASE!?!

ADRIAN CHASE IS DEAD.

NO.

I AM... *THE VIGILANTE!*

I--I'M SORRY ABOUT YOUR WIFE AND KIDS, I REALLY AM. THEY WEREN'T SUPPOSED TO GET HURT...

BELIEVE ME... PLEASE BELIEVE ME.

DON'T HURT ME... I DON'T WANT TO DIE.

I--I'M SORRY ABOUT YOUR FAMILY...

GET UP. ON YOUR FEET. NOW.

OKAY, OKAY... SURE...WHATEVER YOU WANT. BUT PLEASE...DON'T SHOOT.

HE WON'T.

HOW DID YOU KNOW?

THAT *YOU* WERE BEHIND THIS? THAT YOU WERE THE ONE WHO STOPPED SCARAPELLI'S ASSASSINS?

I'M A *DETECTIVE*, CHASE. THAT TAPE YOU SENT *HAD* TO BE MADE *AFTER* SCARAPELLI BOMBED YOUR APARTMENT, NOT BEFORE, LIKE YOU WANTED US TO BELIEVE.

HIS PEOPLE HAD NO REASON TO KILL HIM UNTIL THEN.

SO I KNEW YOU WERE *STILL* IN NEW YORK.

CHASE IS DEAD...

DON'T HAND ME THAT CRUD. I'VE *LIVED* WITH THAT KIND OF THINKING SINCE I WAS A KID.

40

AND WHAT DO YOU WANT FROM ME?

IF YOU *BELIEVE* IN THE LAW LIKE YOU SAY YOU DO, YOU'LL LET ME TAKE SCARAPELLI TO TRIAL.

BUT IF YOU SHOOT HIM, YOU'LL BE AS BAD AS HE IS.

MAYBE...

BAM!

AGHHH!

CHUD-UD-AH!

...BUT... MAYBE NOT...

LATER...

ROBIN? ROBIN, THIS IS WONDER GIRL... COME IN.

ROBIN!?!

41

"...WE INTERRUPT "LENNY AND SQUIGGY GO TO THE WHITE HOUSE" FOR THIS SPECIAL NEWS BULLETIN NOW IN PROGRESS."

REPUTED MOBSTER ANTHONY SCARAPELLI WAS FOUND SHOT TO DEATH IN HIS HOME TONIGHT ALONGSIDE THE WOUNDED BODY OF ROBIN, LEADER OF THE NEW TEEN TITANS.

POLICE CAPTAIN HALL SAID SCARAPELLI HAD SHOT ROBIN, BUT THERE WERE NO CLUES AS TO WHO HAD KILLED SCARAPELLI.

HALL DID SAY, HOWEVER, THAT HE RECEIVED AN ANONYMOUS CALL INFORMING THE POLICE OF THE SHOOTING AND REQUESTING AN AMBULANCE FOR THE WOUNDED TEEN HERO.

WE NOW GO TO CLIVE PHILLIPS AT FLYNN HOSPITAL.

ROBIN, THE POLICE HAVE CLEARED YOU IN SCARAPELLI'S MURDER, BUT THE QUESTION STILL REMAINS--

--DID YOU SEE WHO KILLED HIM?

MR. PHILLIPS, I CAN TRUTHFULLY SAY I WAS ALREADY UNCONSCIOUS BY THE TIME THAT SHOT WAS FIRED.

SO YOUR GUESS IS AS GOOD AS MINE.

AND SO THE MYSTERY STILL REMAINS. WHO KILLED ANTHONY SCARAPELLI? WHO CALLED FOR THE AMBULANCE WHICH SAVED YOUNG ROBIN'S LIFE, AND WHO SENT SCARAPELLI'S PRIVATE DOCU-MENTED RECORDS OF MOB ACTIVITY TO POLICE CAPTAIN HALL?

TRADITIONALLY, SUPER-HEROES SUCH AS SUPERMAN, BATMAN, WONDER WOMAN AND THE TEEN TITANS DO NOT WILLINGLY TAKE LIVES, DO WE NOW HAVE A NEW KIND OF HERO IN TOWN? OR DO WE SIMPLY HAVE YET ANOTHER KILLER ON THE LOOSE? ONLY TIME WILL TELL.

NOW, BACK TO OUR REGULARLY SCHEDULED SHOW...

VIGILANTE JUSTICE

NOT THE END!

42

ROMEO TANGHAL

Born and raised in the Philippines, Romeo Tanghal began drawing comics professionally after graduating from high school. He immigrated to the United States in 1976 and almost immediately began working for DC Comics. A prolific inker and occasional penciller, Tanghal contributed to a vast array of DC's titles over the next 25 years, including JUSTICE LEAGUE OF AMERICA, WONDER WOMAN, GREEN LANTERN and, of course, THE NEW TEEN TITANS.

PABLO MARCOS

One of the best-known Peruvian comics artists of his generation, Pablo Marcos began his art career in the 1960s in his native country drawing caricatures for a political magazine called *Rochabus*. In the 1970s he brought his realistic style to America, where he worked for publishers such as DC, Marvel, Warren and Atlas. He remains active in the industry to this day, contributing recently to *Heavy Metal*, *Frank Frazetta Fantasy Illustrated* and Dynamite Entertainment's *Red Sonja*.

BIOGRAPHIES

MARV WOLFMAN

One of the most prolific and influential writers in modern comics, Marv Wolfman began his career as an artist. Realizing that his talents lay more in writing the stories than in drawing them, he soon became known for his carefully crafted, character-driven tales.

In a career that has spanned more than 30 years, Wolfman has helped shape the heroic sagas of DC Comics' Green Lantern, Blackhawk and the original Teen Titans, as well as Marvel Comics' Fantastic Four, Spider-Man, and Nova. In addition to co-creating THE NEW TEEN TITANS and the universe-shattering CRISIS ON INFINITE EARTHS with George Pérez, Wolfman was instrumental in the revamp of Superman after CRISIS, the development of THE NEW TEEN TITANS spinoff series VIGILANTE, DEATHSTROKE THE TERMINATOR and TEAM TITANS, and created such characters as Blade for Marvel, along with the titles NIGHT FORCE and the retooled DIAL "H" FOR HERO for DC.

In addition to his numerous comic book credits, Wolfman has also written several novels and worked in series television and animation, including the *Superman* cartoon of the late 1980s and the hit *Teen Titans* show on Cartoon Network. His novelization of CRISIS ON INFINITE EARTHS was published in the spring of 2005 by iBooks.

GEORGE PÉREZ

George Pérez started drawing at the age of five and hasn't stopped since. Born on June 9, 1954, Pérez began his professional comics career as an assistant to Rich Buckler in 1973. After establishing himself as a penciller at Marvel Comics, Pérez came to DC in 1980, bringing his highly detailed art style to such titles as JUSTICE LEAGUE OF AMERICA and FIRESTORM. After co-creating THE NEW TEEN TITANS in 1980, Pérez and writer Marv Wolfman reunited for the landmark miniseries CRISIS ON INFINITE EARTHS in 1985. In the aftermath of that universe-smashing event, Pérez revitalized WONDER WOMAN as the series' writer and artist, reestablishing the Amazon Princess as one of DC's preeminent characters and bringing in some of the best sales the title has ever experienced. He has since gone on to illustrate celebrated runs on Marvel's *The Avengers*, CrossGen's *Solus* and DC's THE BRAVE AND THE BOLD. His newest project is *George Pérez's Sirens* for BOOM! Studios.